Who's Afraid of
Postmodernism?

THE CHURCH   *James K. A. Smith, series editor*
AND POSTMODERN
CULTURE

The Church and Postmodern
Culture series features high-profile
theorists in continental philosophy
and contemporary theology
writing for a broad, nonspecialist
audience interested in the impact of
postmodern theory on the faith and
practice of the church.

Forthcoming authors and topics

Bruce Ellis Benson, associate professor of philosophy at
Wheaton College, writes on improvisation as a paradigm
for thinking about worship and the arts

John D. Caputo, David C. Cook Emeritus Professor of
Philosophy at Villanova University and Watson Professor
of Religious Studies at Syracuse University, asks "What
would Jesus deconstruct?"

Graham Ward, professor of contextual theology and ethics at the University of Manchester, writes on political
discipleship

Merold Westphal, distinguished professor of philosophy
at Fordham University, writes on transcendence, community, and interpretation in conversation with Kierkegaard and Levinas

Who's Afraid of
Postmodernism?

*Taking Derrida, Lyotard,
and Foucault to Church*

James K. A. Smith

Baker Academic
Grand Rapids, Michigan

Published by Baker Academic
a division of Baker Publishing Group
P.O. Box 6287, Grand Rapids, MI 49516-6287
www.bakeracademic.com

Printed in the United States of America

Library of Congress Cataloging-in-Publication Data
Smith, James K. A., 1970–
    Who's afraid of postmodernism? : taking Derrida, Lyotard, and
Foucault to church / James K. A. Smith.
        p.   cm. — (The church and postmodern culture)
    Includes bibliographical references (p.   ) and index.
    ISBN 10: 0-8010-2918-X (pbk.)
    ISBN 978-0-8010-2918-9 (pbk.)
    1. Postmodernism—Religious aspects—Christianity. 2. Christianity—
Philosophy. 3. Derrida, Jacques. 4. Lyotard, Jean François. 5. Foucault,
Michel. I. Title. II. Series.
    BR115.P74S66 2006
    261.5′1—dc22   2005033865

For Coleson,
whose dreams and visions of a fantastic world
encourage me to hope for a re-imagined church

Contents

Series Preface

Current discussions in the church—from emergent "postmodern" congregations to mainline "missional" congregations—are increasingly grappling with philosophical and theoretical questions related to postmodernity. In fact, it could be argued that developments in postmodern theory (especially questions of "post-foundationalist" epistemologies) have contributed to the breakdown of former barriers between evangelical, mainline, and Catholic faith communities. Postliberalism—a related "effect" of postmodernism—has engendered a new, confessional ecumenism wherein we find nondenominational evangelical congregations, mainline Protestant churches, and Catholic parishes all wrestling with the challenges of postmodernism and drawing on the culture of postmodernity as an *opportunity* for rethinking the shape of our churches.

This context presents an exciting opportunity for contemporary philosophy and critical theory to "hit the ground," so to speak, by allowing high-level work in postmodern theory to serve the church's practice—including all the kinds of congregations and communions noted above. The goal of this series is to bring together high-profile theorists in continental philosophy and contemporary theology to write for a broad, nonspecialist audience interested in the impact of postmodern theory on the faith and practice of the church. Each book in the series will, from different angles and with different questions, undertake to answer questions such as What does postmodern theory have to say about the shape of the church? How should concrete, in-the-pew and on-the-ground religious practices be impacted by postmodernism? What should the church look like in postmodernity? What has Paris to do with Jerusalem?

The series is ecumenical not only with respect to its ecclesial destinations but also with respect to the facets of continental philosophy and theory that are represented. A wide variety of theoretical commitments will be included, ranging from deconstruction to Radical Orthodoxy, including voices from Badiou to Žižek and the usual suspects in between (Nietzsche, Heidegger, Levinas, Derrida, Foucault, Irigaray, Rorty, and others). Insofar as postmodernism occasions a retrieval of ancient sources, these contemporary sources will be brought into dialogue with Augustine, Irenaeus, Aquinas, and other resources. Drawing on the wisdom of established scholars in the field, the series will provide accessible introductions to postmodern thought with the specific aim of exploring its impact on ecclesial practice. The books are offered, one might say, as French lessons for the church.

Preface

To the Reader

A word about my intended audience and modus operandi: Although I wish seriously to engage philosophical currents and ideas (in the way Francis Schaeffer faced ideas head-on) and am a philosopher by both profession and training (though also engaged in ministry for the past dozen years), in this book I am writing not primarily to philosophers or theologians (though they might find it of interest) but rather to students and practitioners—to those trying to orient themselves to the issues and those on the front lines of cultural engagement in the postmodern world: pastors and youth pastors, campus ministers and worship leaders, clergy and laypersons, and those training for such vocations. Given its original context at L'Abri, the book also speaks to spiritual seekers trying to navigate the postmodern terrain while searching for meaning. To them I want to suggest that, quite unlike the anti-institutional mentality of postmodern "spirituality," it is actually a robust, vibrant, liturgical church that speaks meaning in and to a postmodern world. With these audiences in mind, I have not assumed any philosophical knowledge and have avoided becoming bogged down in textual exposition. Although it is important to trace ideas to their source and listen to theorists firsthand, I have minimized footnotes and citations and concentrated on the ideas and claims being made. Of course, sources and engagement with other literature could be multiplied almost ad infinitum. But rather than distract the reader with extensive footnotes, I have included a bibliography for further reading, which will also point interested readers to my more scholarly discussions of these matters.

Acknowledgments

This book came to me, its author, as a gift—as a wonderful effulgence at the intersection of two very deep, rich streams: the heritage of the Calvin College department of philosophy and the tradition of L'Abri Fellowship in Switzerland. The core of the book was initially presented as a series of lectures in the summer of 2003 at L'Abri, the study center founded by Francis and Edith Schaeffer. The opportunity to give the lectures arose from a working relationship between Calvin's philosophy department and L'Abri that regularly takes Calvin faculty and students to Switzerland. I am very grateful to the philosophy department, particularly Lee Hardy, for the opportunity to go to L'Abri, and to the generous hospitality of Jim and Gail Ingram and the folks at L'Abri for welcoming my wife, Deanna, and me. Both the faculty and the students at L'Abri provided thoughtful questions and insights that have helped me to clarify my thinking on the matters examined in this book.

Throughout my preparation for those lectures, I had a keen sense of being a dwarf standing on the shoulders of giants. On the one hand, the opportunity to present those lectures was a chance to repay a debt. I find myself on the path of Christian philosophy today because of an encounter with the work of Francis Schaeffer when I was a sophomore in college. To be able to carry on that tradition of philosophical reflection, cultural analysis, and biblical discernment in the original lectures and now in this book is an attempt to render thanks and honor to Schaeffer's legacy—even if I might take that legacy in directions that Schaeffer would not. On the other hand, I count myself blessed to be part of the legacy of philosophy at Calvin College, drawing on the stream of tradition handed down from figures like Jellema, Runner, Mouw, Plantinga, and Wolterstorff. And I feel a special sense of gratitude to my contemporary colleagues in the department, who have welcomed me and encouraged me in my labors.

The transformation of the original lectures into a book has also profited from the generosity of several friends who took the time to read the manuscript and offer their comments and criticisms, which have undoubtedly improved it, except in those places where I was too stubborn to listen. My thanks to John Franke, Brian McLaren, Bill VanGroningen, and Geoff Holsclaw for this very tangible expression of friendship.

Finally, I owe much to my family for their unflagging support and for keeping me rooted in the realities of faith and practice. This book brings back special memories of an adventure with Deanna in Switzerland and France that I shall never forget and shall always cherish. The challenge of raising children in a postmodern culture is what spurs many of my concerns in this book, particularly the reflections on the formation of desire in chapter 4. I dedicate this book to my second son, Coleson, whose passion for Tolkien, King Arthur, and things medieval spurs my own ancient-future sensibilities. My prayer is that he will keep seeking the Grail.

⚜

Some of the material in chapters 2 and 3 appeared in an earlier form in *Christianity and the Postmodern Turn: Six Views*, ed. Myron B. Penner (Grand Rapids: Brazos, 2005) and is included here with the kind permission of the editor and publisher.

1

Is the Devil from Paris?

Postmodernism and the Church

> Postmodernism tends to be something of a cha-
> meleon, portrayed as either monster or savior—ei-
> ther the new form of the enemy or the next best
> thing to come along. This chapter introduces the
> questions that the phenomenon of postmodernism
> poses for the church and suggests a strategy for
> engagement that avoids simple dichotomies of
> either demonizing or baptizing postmodernism.

Raising the Curtain: *The Matrix*

"Welcome to the *real* world."[1] With these words, Neo is welcomed by Morpheus after emerging from his imprisonment in
the matrix, a "neural-active simulation complex" designed by
machines to control human beings. Although Neo escapes from
the trappings of a postapocalyptic world, the scene in fact replays
one of the most ancient of philosophical images: emerging from

1. *The Matrix*, DVD, written and directed by Andy and Larry Wachowski
(Burbank, CA: Warner Home Video, 1999).

Plato's cave. In Plato's *Republic*, Socrates recounts the way in which the masses are enslaved to a world of images and shadows, as though chained in the depths of a cave, their heads locked in position. Because of these restraints, all they have ever seen are the shadows dancing on the cave wall, cast by a small fire that sends light across the puppets and artifacts carried along a wall behind them. Never knowing anything different, each of the cave's prisoners considers the shadows real, until one of them is released. Turning from the wall of shadows, this liberated prisoner begins to make his way out of the cave, steadily proceeding toward the world above. Immediately upon turning around, he realizes that the shadows are only images cast by the puppets and cutouts behind him. Moving past these and past the cave's interior fire, the prisoner slowly emerges from his subterranean confinement into the light of day and the world above.

At first the experience is bewildering and bedazzling; the sun's light blinds eyes accustomed only to darkness. Indeed, the light of the real world is painful to eyes that have not seen it. Unable to look up at first, the liberated prisoner must navigate his way around the world by looking at shadows on the ground and images in the water. But these images are cast not by copies and cutouts but by the things themselves. Indeed, the experience of emerging from the cave has slowly revealed that what the prisoner had thought was real was in fact but a shadow of reality, a copy of a copy. In the world above he could behold not just the shadow of a tree, nor even the cutout image of a tree, but the tree itself. What would have seemed ludicrous to him before his liberation—that the world of his birth, his entire environment was not real—was now clear. Clearer still is what the prisoner must now do: return to the cave, liberate his companions, and proclaim the truth of what is real.

The figure of Neo in the Wachowski brothers' *Matrix* is a postmodern Platonic prisoner. He has spent his entire life in a prison of sorts, a pod of quasi-uterine liquid where he is nourished by hoses, and dancing before his consciousness is not a dim, darkened world of shadows but a Technicolor reality of high-rises and coffee shops, computers and nightclubs. The "wall" on which all of this is played out is within Neo's own mind, where a "neural-active simulation" program feeds a world of images directly into his consciousness. Thus, though these human prisoners are actually trapped in pods where they are "harvested" for energy to run AI, they believe themselves to be someone and somewhere else. While Neo's body is hooked up to a system of cords and hoses, he thinks that he is one Thomas Anderson, a mediocre employee of a growing technology firm.

Morpheus comes to Neo as a liberator, someone who knows the truth and can thus descend into the depths of the cave's darkness in order to liberate others. Although Morpheus meets Neo in the matrix, he and his crew are able to effect the release of his body—his real self—from the pod. When his questioning mind no longer receives the neural-active simulation that is the matrix (something like a body rejecting a transplanted organ), the system flushes him out of the pod as waste. Morpheus and his crew seize Neo, lifting him from the dark dungeon toward the luminous light of reality, dramatized by his body being hoisted from the dark caverns up toward the tunnel of light shining from the ship *Nebuchadnezzar*. When Neo awakes, Morpheus greets him: "Welcome to the real world." Slipping in and out of consciousness, Neo asks: "Why do my eyes hurt?" "Because you've never used them before" is the reply. This lack of use requires a rigorous regimen of rehabilitation. Spitting out a stream of questions and receiving a barrage of dizzying answers, Neo experiences a kind of vertigo and vomits out of disorientation. It's not easy getting used to the real world.

Our contemporary culture, including the church, has experienced a similar dis- and reorientation. This book focuses on a transition not unlike that experienced by Neo: an emerging from one place to another, from one construction of reality to another, from modernity to postmodernity. While we might not name it as such, our experience of cultural shifts and changes can be traced to the advent of postmodernity and the trickle-down effect of postmodernism on our popular culture. The transition calls into question almost all our previously held sureties and rattles a faith that has been too easily equated with such Cartesian "certainties," sometimes issuing in a kind of vertigo. Like Neo's experience, our emergence into this new situation engenders a host of questions and a confused sense of being lost. As Morpheus puts it to Neo, whose mind is swirling in this new reality: "I imagine right now you must feel a bit like Alice, tumbling down the rabbit hole." Or as W. H. Auden once described this kind of cultural upheaval,

"It's as if we had left our house for five minutes to mail a letter, and during that time the living room had changed places with the room behind the mirror over the fireplace."[2] If the shadows we thought were real have been unveiled as mere shadows, doesn't it sometimes feel as if the whole world were dissolving? Even if we have a sense that this is "the real world," as Morpheus announces, we're not sure how to make our way in it.

While I don't want to claim the mantle of Morpheus, my hope is to offer a kind of therapy and rehabilitation, an orientation to the world of postmodernism, which is simply to say, the world in which we now find ourselves.

What Is Postmodernism?

The notion of postmodernism is invoked as both poison and cure within the contemporary church. To some, postmodernity is the bane of Christian faith, the new enemy taking over the role of secular humanism as object of fear and primary target of demonization.[3] Others see postmodernism as a fresh wind of the Spirit sent to revitalize the dry bones of the church.[4] This is particularly true of the "emerging church" movement (associated with Brian McLaren, Leonard Sweet, Robert Webber, and others), which castigates the modernity of pragmatic evangelicalism and seeks to retool the church's witness for a postmodern world. In both cases, however, postmodernism remains a nebulous

2. W. H. Auden, "If, on account of the Political Situation," from *The Complete Works of W. H. Auden* (Princeton, NJ: Princeton University Press, 1988).
3. See, for instance, Charles Colson, "The Postmodern Crackup: From Soccer Moms to College Campuses, Signs of the End," *Christianity Today,* December 2003, 72. See also the work of Millard Erickson, Douglas Groothuis, and D. A. Carson (*The Gagging of God: Christianity Confronts Pluralism* [Grand Rapids: Zondervan, 1996] and *Becoming Conversant with the Emerging Church: Understanding a Movement and Its Implications* [Grand Rapids: Zondervan, 2005]).
4. See, for instance, Brian D. McLaren, *A New Kind of Christian: A Tale of Two Friends on a Spiritual Journey* (San Francisco: Jossey-Bass, 2001); idem, *The Church on the Other Side: Doing Ministry in the Postmodern Matrix* (Grand Rapids: Zondervan, 2000); Leonard Sweet, *SoulTsunami: Sink or Swim in New Millennium Culture* (Grand Rapids: Zondervan, 1999); Robert E. Webber, *The Younger Evangelicals: Facing the Challenges of the New World* (Grand Rapids: Baker, 2002); and Carl Raschke, *The Next Reformation: Why Evangelicals Must Embrace Postmodernity* (Grand Rapids: Baker, 2004).

concept—a slippery beast eluding our understanding. Or perhaps better, postmodernism tends to be a chameleon taking on whatever characteristics we want it to: if it is seen as enemy, postmodernism will be defined as monstrous; if it is seen as savior, postmodernism will be defined as redemptive. This ambiguity tends to make us—Christian scholars, pastors and ministers, laypersons engaged in ministry—skeptical about just what we're talking about. *What is postmodernism?*

The answer to this question is sometimes offered as a historical thesis: postmodernism has been variously described as a kind of *post-* (after-) modern condition and is sometimes even linked to particular historical events such as student riots in 1968, the abandonment of the gold standard, the fall of the Berlin Wall, or, to be specific, 3:32 p.m. on July 15, 1972![5] Each candidate for the advent of postmodernism relies on an account of the supposed collapse of modernity. Trying to pinpoint the advent of the postmodern condition by linking it to a historical epoch, particular event, or even a particular cultural sphere (architecture, literature, music, visual arts) seems counterproductive, given the widespread disagreement about such historical claims. Further, it seems naïve to think that a *Zeitgeist* like postmodernism could be spawned by a single event.

Instead of trying to pinpoint its historical origin or essence, I want to unpack an assumption that most commentators on postmodernism seem to share in common: postmodernism, whether monster or savior, is something that has come slouching out of Paris. In particular, postmodernism owes its impetus to French philosophical influences. While most commentators from various disciplines (architecture, art, literature, theology) concede this point, few have facility with philosophy or French philosophy in particular. In other words, we tend to give French philosophy a nod as crucial for understanding postmodernism but then do not engage the philosophical underpinnings. Brian McLaren, for instance, regularly tips his hat to the philosophical but then pushes it aside as "too far removed from everyday life" or not nec-

5. This is when the Pruitt-Ingoe housing development (a prize-winning version of Le Corbusier's "machine for modern living") in St. Louis was dynamited as an uninhabitable environment for the low-income people it housed. See Charles Jencks, *Le Corbusier and the Continual Revolution in Architecture* (New York: Monacelli, 2000).

essary for understanding "postmodernity" as distinguished from "philosophical postmodernism."[6] But I want to follow Francis Schaeffer's footsteps by taking philosophy very seriously precisely because it does impact everyday life. "Ideas have legs," and even in a culture of amusement, there is thought that shapes it.

As Schaeffer remarks in the foreword to *Escape from Reason*, "If we are to understand present-day trends in thought, we must see how the situation has come about historically and also look in some detail at the development of philosophic thought-forms."[7] In *The God Who Is There*, Schaeffer analyzes the shifts of modernity as beginning with philosophy (the "first step" in the "line of despair"); thus cultural phenomena, for Schaeffer, are symptoms of philosophical shifts, not vice versa. In his critical cultural analyses as found in *The God Who Is There* or *Escape from Reason*, Schaeffer offers what we might call a trickle-down theory of philosophical influence: cultural phenomena tend to eventually reflect philosophical movements. Perhaps my analyses of philosophical postmodernism can be understood as a necessary supplement (or better, prerequisite) to McLaren's analyses of postmodernity.[8]

Thus in this book I want to employ a Schaefferian strategy in considering postmodernism.[9] As such, I consider it a sequel to

6. McLaren, *Church on the Other Side*, 160; and idem, *New Kind of Christian*, 19.

7. Schaeffer, *Escape from Reason*, in *The Francis A. Schaeffer Trilogy* (Westchester, IL: Crossway, 1990), 208.

8. While I can't pursue this in detail, we should at least note a common heuristic distinction between postmodernism as an intellectual movement and postmodernity as a constellation of cultural phenomena. Derrida's deconstruction and Foucault's genealogy of power are examples of postmoder*nism*; adolescent absorption in virtual reality and the triumph of the mall as temple are examples of postmoder*nity*. Although there is a trickle-down effect between philosophical currents of postmodernism and cultural phenomena related to postmodernity, much that is associated with cultural postmodernity is, in fact, the fruit of modernity. In other words, cultural phenomena tend to not (yet?) reflect the radical implications of postmodernism. This might be because postmodernism itself has shrunk back from its own implications in both intellectual and cultural spheres. The individualism and consumerism that characterize contemporary culture are fruit nourished by deeply modern roots. So also relativism owes much more to modernism than to postmodernism. In this book, I focus primarily on the intellectual currents of postmodernism, but there remain important questions about cultural phenomena that could be rightly described as postmodern.

9. McLaren also looks to Schaeffer as a prototype in this regard. He cites Schaeffer's exhortation to the church a generation ago: "One of the greatest

Schaeffer's own engagements with humanism and existentialism; postmodernism (a term rarely used in France, by the way) is, in some sense, the heir to existentialism. By a Schaefferian strategy, I mean at least two things: first, we need to return to the philosophy itself to understand postmodernity. While postmodernity as a cultural phenomenon is often distinguished from postmodernism as a philosophical movement, I agree with Schaeffer that cultural phenomena tend to be a product of philosophical movements. We take culture seriously by taking ideas seriously. Second, my strategy is "Schaefferian" in the sense that my primary audience is not just philosophers but practitioners—more specifically, Christians engaged in ministry in a postmodern world, as well as searching inhabitants of this postmodern world. As such, these essays are not an academic project per se. Instead, their purpose is to introduce philosophical currents to people who don't usually travel that stream. Thus I avoid philosophical jargon as much as possible. Where special terminology is necessary, it is couched in a context of explanation and clarification. I see this as an *incarnational* strategy, attempting to accommodate thought to language that is accessible to an audience, just as Calvin so often emphasized that God in Christ accommodates his thought to our language, appearing as a Word that we can understand.[10]

With the humble goal of trying to unpack the primary philosophical impulses behind postmodernism, my strategy is to engage something of an unholy trinity of postmodern thinkers: Jacques Derrida, Jean-François Lyotard, and Michel Foucault. While their names might not be familiar to everyone, key aspects of their thought have now become commonplace not just in the academy but in the media as well. In particular, I carefully consider three slogans of postmodernism associated with these philosophers:

- "There is nothing outside the text" (Derrida).

---

injustices we do to our young people is to ask them to be conservative. . . . If we want to be fair, we must teach the young to be revolutionaries, revolutionaries against the status quo" (McLaren, *Church on the Other Side*, 16).

10. I have explored the notion of incarnational language more fully in my *Speech and Theology: Language and the Logic of Incarnation*, Radical Orthodoxy Series (London: Routledge, 2002).

- Postmodernity is "incredulity toward metanarratives" (Lyotard).
- "Power is knowledge" (Foucault).

Generally, these three slogans are invoked as being mutually exclusive to confessional Christian faith. How could someone who takes the sweeping narrative of the Scriptures as the Word of God reject metanarratives? How could someone who believes in the existence of a transcendent God and his creation deny that there is reality outside texts? How could someone who worships the God who is Love participate in a Nietzschean celebration of the will to power as the basis of reality?

The problem is that all these questions are rooted in a misunderstanding of the claims being made. In other words, these slogans (which were never intended as slogans by their authors) are treated like bumper stickers: claims made without a context. Once we appreciate the context of these claims, however, we see two things: First, they mean something different than what the "bumper-sticker" reading suggests. The bumper-sticker readings that turn these claims into slogans tend to perpetuate a number of myths about postmodernism. My goal is to demythologize postmodernism by showing that what we commonly think so-called postmodernists are saying is usually not the case. Second, and perhaps more provocatively, I will demonstrate that, in fact, all these claims have a deep affinity with central Christian claims.

As such, the studies that make up chapters 2–4 are intended to function as a two-edged sword. On the one hand, I critically introduce Christians to currents in contemporary thought, often described as postmodernism. This requires subjecting these ideas to criticism from an integrally Christian worldview. But they are also meant to cut the other way as well; that is, I also critique common Christian misunderstandings of postmodernism and suggest ways in which postmodernity is a condition that Christians should, in some sense, welcome. Something good *can* come out of Paris. In this way, I'm simply replaying a Hebrew strategy, later adopted by Augustine and utilized by the likes of John Calvin and Abraham Kuyper: making off with Egyptian loot. As Augustine put it in his *Teaching Christianity* (*De doctrina christiana*), just as the Hebrews left Egypt with Egyptian gold to be put to use in the worship of Yahweh (even if they misdirected its use at times), so Christians can find resources in non-Christian thought—whether that of Plato or of Derrida—that can be put to work for the glory of God and the furtherance of the kingdom. This book is an attempt to make off with postmodern loot for the sake of the kingdom.

In particular, I suggest that this unholy trinity of Derrida, Lyotard, and Foucault might in fact push us to recapture some truths about the nature of the church that have been overshadowed by modernity and especially by Christian appropriations of modernism. One of the reasons postmodernism has been the bogeyman for the Christian church is that we have become so thoroughly modern. But while postmodernism may be the enemy of our modernity, it can be an ally of our ancient heritage. In short, it might just be these Parisians who can help us *be* the church. Specifically, each of the analyses made by these postmodern theorists entails a twofold effect for the church:

- *Derrida.* Deconstruction's claim that there is "nothing outside the text" [*il n'y a pas de hors-texte*] can be considered a radical translation of the Reformation principle *sola scriptura*. In particular, Derrida's insight should push us to recover two key emphases of the church: (a) the centrality of Scripture for mediating our understanding of the world as a whole and (b) the role of community in the interpretation of Scripture.
- *Lyotard.* The assertion that postmodernity is "incredulity toward metanarratives" is ultimately a claim to be affirmed by the church, pushing us to recover (a) the narrative character of Christian faith, rather than understanding it as a collection of ideas, and (b) the confessional nature of our narrative and the way in which we find ourselves in a world of competing narratives.
- *Foucault.* The seemingly disturbing, even Nietzschean claim that "power is knowledge" should push us to realize what MTV learned long ago: (a) the cultural power of formation and discipline, and hence (b) the necessity of the church to enact counterformation by counterdisciplines. In other words, we need to think about discipline as a creational

structure that needs proper direction. Foucault has something to tell us about what it means to be a disciple.

Of course, since none of these theorists are Christians, we should also expect some points of fundamental disagreement as well as the necessity to critique some of their conclusions.

Each chapter employs a common strategy to open up these postmodern thinkers and theories and begins with a brief discussion of a recent film as a way of illustrating some of the questions and issues at stake. Film is the new lingua franca of not just American culture but, increasingly, global culture. Further, it is a powerful "incarnational" medium that can reveal truth about our world, opening up our experience in a way that propositions and textbooks cannot. The film discussions, then, are intended to activate our curiosity—to get us asking the kinds of questions that these postmodern theorists are asking. Then, I introduce the central claim made by each figure, explaining what is being said by considering the context of the claim in the author's work. This will then require some clarification, particularly in the face of common misunderstandings of the claim, especially by Christian theologians and practitioners. We'll then explore the implications of this claim for the church, in both its theology and its practice (the two should never be separated), leading up to a constructive conclusion regarding the shape of the postmodern church.

Thus, each chapter ends with a "tour" of a postmodern church. After considering the thought of Derrida, Lyotard, and Foucault, each chapter concludes with a case study, considering recent developments in the church that have attempted to respond to the postmodern condition, such as the emerging church movement. In the work of Brian McLaren, Leonard Sweet, and others, we find Christian thinkers and practitioners who have specifically tried to engage the cultural shift to postmodernity. These bold explorers have been some of the first to map the postmodern terrain for the church. Given our engagement with the key theorists of postmodernity, we'll critically consider both their reading of postmodernism as well as their proposals for the shape of the postmodern church. As will become clear, although I share a deep sympathy with their concerns, I also think that at times their proposals remain captive to some modernist strategies.[11] I will argue that the postmodern church could do nothing better than be ancient, that the most powerful way to reach a postmodern world is by recovering tradition, and that the most effective means of discipleship is found in liturgy. Each tour of a postmodern church will give a concrete picture of what Derrida, Lyotard, and Foucault might mean for how we worship.

A thoughtful engagement with postmodernism will encourage us to look backward. We will see that much that goes under the banner of postmodern philosophy has one eye on ancient and medieval sources and constitutes a significant recovery of premodern ways of knowing, being, and doing. Ancient and medieval sources provide a useful countervoice to modernity.[12] Thus Derrida constantly engages Plato (and later, Augustine), Lyotard looks at tribal cultures, and Foucault considers ancient practices of discipline. Without being conservative or trying to recover a (mythical) pristine tradition in the name of "paleo-orthodoxy," postmodernism does stage a certain creative recovery of ancient themes and figures.[13] The three studies that make up chapters 2–4 set the stage for a concluding chapter that makes the case that the most persistent postmodernism should issue in a thickly confessional church that draws on the very particular (yet catholic) and ancient practices of the church's worship and discipleship. In other words, a "radical orthodoxy" is the only proper outcome of the postmodern critique, and insofar as the emerging church shrinks from an unapologetic dogmatics (which isn't a rabid fundamentalism), it remains captive to the dreams, ambitions, and skepticism of modernity. Thus chapter 5 considers why the best way to be postmodern is to be ancient, and the best way to proclaim Christian faith in the postmodern world is not quietly,

11. For example, "nondenominationalism" might be seen as a deeply modern phenomenon. I discuss this further in chapter 4.

12. This resonance between ancient and postmodern thought has been suggested by medieval scholar David Burrell, who notes the affinity between postmodernism and medieval theology. "Postmodern," he suggests, "could be translated as 'anti-antimedieval'" (in *Faith and Freedom: An Interfaith Perspective* [Oxford: Blackwell, 2004], 141).

13. Many, I suspect, would be surprised to know that Parisian philosophical circles are currently abuzz with discussions of Saint Augustine, led by the work of Jean-Luc Marion at the Sorbonne.

with a chastised timidity, but unapologetically, with an embodied commitment to justice in community.[14]

Apologetics and Witness in a Postmodern World

Talking about "postmodernism" can give the impression that we are describing a discrete, specific phenomenon, like a table or a cup. Further, one is tempted to suggest that with the advent of postmodernity, everything has changed. But neither of these is true: Postmodernism is an admittedly pluriform and variegated phenomenon. And postmodernism does not make a clean break from modernism. There are both continuities and discontinuities between modernity and postmodernity. The most significant continuity is that both deny grace; in other words, both modernity and postmodernity are characterized by an idolatrous notion of self-sufficiency and a deep naturalism.[15] Noting this theological continuity, one also recognizes philosophical and cultural continuities, such that postmodernity is often an intensification of modernity, particularly with respect to notions of freedom, the use of technology, and so on.

These continuities influence the discussion that follows in two ways: First, I tend to emphasize the discontinuities between modernity and postmodernity. I recognize—and have argued elsewhere—that there are deep continuities between modern and postmodern thought, particularly in the work of Derrida and Foucault, both of whom confess that they are, in an important sense, Enlightenment thinkers.[16] However, there is also an important sense in which they are critics of modernity, and thus postmodernism does in some way break with modernism. In the analyses presented in this book, I am particularly interested in

14. My thinking along these lines owes much to Robert Webber, *Ancient-Future Faith: Rethinking Evangelicalism for a Postmodern World* (Grand Rapids: Baker, 1999).

15. Or as Graham Hughes suggests, both modernity and postmodernity are characterized by a trenchant "disenchantment of the world," to use Max Weber's phrase (Hughes, *Worship as Meaning: A Liturgical Theology for Late Modernity* [Cambridge: Cambridge University Press, 2003], 2).

16. See, for example, James K. A. Smith, *Jacques Derrida: Live Theory* (London: Continuum, 2005), 3.3.2.

the opportunities that this rupture represents for recapturing a more robust—and less modern—Christian faith.

This leads to my second emphasis on the continuities between postmodernism and orthodox Christian faith.[17] Much in the work of Derrida, Lyotard, and Foucault merits criticism, especially from a Christian perspective. Here, and in the context of the original lectures that make up this book, however, it seemed necessary to emphasize points of overlap between postmodernism and historic, orthodox Christian faith, especially because I am, in some sense, carrying on the Schaefferian legacy. To do so, it is necessary to confront a latent modernism in Schaeffer's own construal of Christian faith as a "system of truth."[18] Rather than explicitly critique Schaeffer on this score, I want to demonstrate that, perhaps to Schaeffer's surprise (and chagrin), the claims of postmodernists such as Derrida and Foucault have something in common with his own account of knowledge and truth (insofar as Schaeffer recognized the role of presuppositions).[19] While Schaeffer generally focused on pointing out the discontinuities

17. I generally use this term as a shorthand to refer to Christian faith as rooted in the Scriptures and attested in the historic creeds and confessions, which I take to be amplified by later Reformed thought. While my project here is quite ecumenical, it will become clear that I think the Reformed confessions are an important extension of historic, orthodox Christian faith. I don't wish to engage in polemics about that here, except insofar as it impacts epistemology (the theory of knowledge) and hence apologetics. And in the end, what is at stake here is an Augustinian catholic theology.

18. See the appendix on "Apologetics" in *Trilogy*.

19. This question is debated, and it seems that even when he explicitly addressed it, Schaeffer remained ambiguous on this score, at times leaning toward a more classical approach that does not take seriously the role of presuppositions in knowledge. Schaeffer's own Reformed theology undercuts classical apologetics insofar as it is committed to the "noetic effects of sin"—that is, the effects of sin on the mind, distorting both what counts as true and what can be recognized as true for the unbeliever (Rom. 1:18–22; 1 Cor. 2). During my stay at L'Abri, I had occasion to look carefully at the classic seventeenth-century work of John Owen on the Holy Spirit. I could recommend no better statement on the noetic effects of sin than his account of "Corruption of the depravity of the mind by sin" (III.iii; *The Holy Spirit* [repr., Grand Rapids: Kregel, 1954], 144–69). One finds the same point articulated in Kierkegaard's *Philosophical Fragments*: in order to come to know the truth, the learner (disciple) must receive from the Teacher (God) not only the content of the truth but also the very condition for receiving it. The dispensation of the condition is an act of grace by the work of the Holy Spirit.

between, say, existentialism and Christian faith, there is a virtue to finding the "point of tension" by also finding the point of contact between Christian and non-Christian thought. And recognizing such a continuity may require that we jettison some of our own modern presuppositions. Our Christian faith—and correlatively, our account of apologetics—is tainted by modernism when we fail to appreciate the effects of sin on reason. When this is ignored, we adopt an Enlightenment optimism about the role of a supposedly neutral reason in the recognition of truth.[20] (We also end up committed to "Constantinian" strategies that, under the banner of natural law, seek to build a "Christian America.")

To put this in more familiar terms, classical apologetics operates with a very modern notion of reason; "presuppositional" apologetics, on the other hand, is postmodern (and Augustinian!) insofar as it recognizes the role of presuppositions in both what counts as truth and what is recognized as true. For this reason, postmodernism can be a catalyst for the church to reclaim its faith not as a system of truth dictated by a neutral reason but rather as a story that requires "eyes to see and ears to hear." The primary responsibility of the church as witness, then, is not demonstration but rather proclamation—the kerygmatic vocation of proclaiming the Word made flesh rather than the thin realities of theism that a supposedly neutral reason yields.

To put it another way, unless our apologetic proclamation begins from revelation, we have conceded the game to modernity. On this score, I side with an even earlier Parisian philosopher and proto-postmodernist, Blaise Pascal, who adamantly protested that the God revealed in the incarnation and the Scriptures—the God of Abraham, Isaac, and Jesus Christ—is to be distinguished from the (modern) god of philosophical theism. But even more importantly, this new apologetic—which is, in fact, ancient—is one that is proclaimed by a community's way of life.[21] As Peter

---

20. In the contemporary context, what I have elsewhere called the "Biola school" of apologetics and Christian philosophy embodies this modernism. For a brief account, see James K. A. Smith, "Who's Afraid of Postmodernism? A Response to the 'Biola School,'" in *Christianity and the Postmodern Turn*, ed. Myron Penner (Grand Rapids: Brazos, 2005).

21. For further discussion of this new apologetic (following Robert Webber), see James K. A. Smith, *Introducing Radical Orthodoxy: Mapping a Post-secular Theology* (Grand Rapids: Baker, 2004), 179–82.

Leithart has remarked, "The first and chief defense of the gospel, the first 'letter of commendation' not only for Paul but for Jesus, is not an argument but the life of the church conformed to Christ by the Spirit in service and suffering."[22] The church doesn't *have* an apologetic; it *is* an apologetic.

From Modern Christianity to a Postmodern Church

If I am opposed to the epistemology, or theory of knowledge, that plagues modern Christianity, then I am also opposed to the ecclesiology (or lack thereof) that accompanies this modernist version of the faith. Within the matrix of a modern Christianity, the base "ingredient" is the individual; the church, then, is simply a collection of individuals. Conceiving of Christian faith as a private affair between the individual and God—a matter of my asking Jesus to "come into my heart"—modern evangelicalism finds it hard to articulate just how or why the church has any role to play other than providing a place to fellowship with other individuals who have a private relationship with God. With this model in place, what matters is Christianity as a system of truth or ideas, not the church as a living community embodying its head. Modern Christianity tends to think of the church either as a place where individuals come to find answers to their questions or as one more stop where individuals can try to satisfy their consumerist desires. As such, Christianity becomes intellectualized rather than incarnate, commodified rather than the site of genuine community.

In discussing Christian faith emerging from modernity to postmodernity, however, I rarely speak of Christianity, and I even resist talking about Christians as individuals; rather, I tend to speak of the church—indeed, with a capital *C*. I want to advocate a shift from modern Christianity to a postmodern church, one akin to the paradigm shift experienced by Neo. My point here is confessional: as attested in the Apostles' Creed, I believe in the holy catholic church, and I believe that the very notion of the holy catholic church undoes the modern individualism that

22. Peter J. Leithart, *Against Christianity* (Moscow, ID: Canon, 2003), 99.

plagues contemporary evangelicalism.[23] Indeed, we would do well to recover a much-maligned formula: "There is no salvation outside the church." This doesn't mean that a particular ecclesial body is the dispenser of grace or the arbiter of salvation; rather, there simply is no Christianity apart from the body of Christ, which is the church. The body is the New Testament's organic model of community that counters the modernist emphasis on the individual.

The church does not exist *for* me; my salvation is not primarily a matter of intellectual mastery or emotional satisfaction. The church is the site where God renews and transforms us—a place where the practices of being the body of Christ form us into the image of the Son. What I, a sinner saved by grace, need is not so much answers as reformation of my will and heart. What I describe as the practices of the church include the traditional sacramental[24] practices of baptism and Eucharist but also the practices of Christian marriage and child-rearing, even the simple but radical practices of friendship and being called to get along with those one doesn't like! The church, for instance, is a place to learn patience by practice. The fruit of the Spirit emerges in our lives from the seeds planted by the practices of being the church; and when the church begins to exhibit the fruit of the Spirit, it becomes a witness to a postmodern world (John 17). Nothing is more countercultural than a community serving the Suffering Servant in a world devoted to consumption and violence. But the church will have this countercultural, prophetic witness only when it jettisons its own modernity; in that respect postmodernism can be another catalyst for the church to *be* the church.

---

23. I remain concerned that, despite all of the talk about community in the emerging church, we have not yet explored the radical implications of it. The next task for the emerging church is to articulate an ecclesiology.

24. Here we do well to return to the rich, sacramental theology of John Calvin as opposed to the thin, Zwinglian theologies that seem to have won the day in Reformed evangelical circles.

2

Nothing outside the Text?

Derrida, Deconstruction, and Scripture

If postmodernism has anything close to a brand name, it is deconstruction, and if it has anything like a celebrity face, it is the dark face of a Parisian transplanted from North Africa: the face of Jacques Derrida. In this chapter we will consider the central themes of deconstruction through one of Derrida's most (in)famous claims: "There is nothing outside the text."

Raising the Curtain: *Memento*

Lenny has a problem.[1] Well, he has lots of problems—believe me!—but one stands out: he can't remember what he did five minutes ago. Since a tragic incident involving the death of his wife, Lenny has not been able to make new memories. He can remember everything from *before* the accident and thus can remember where he's from and how to navigate his way through

1. *Memento*, DVD, written and directed by Christopher Nolan (Culver City, CA: Columbia TriStar Home Entertainment, 2001).

day-to-day life: how to eat, how to drive, and very importantly, how to *write*.[2] But while he's driving, he can't remember why he got in the car. Or when he enters a restaurant, he can't remember why he came. When he goes to meet a recent acquaintance, he can't remember what she looks like. And as the motel manager quickly figures out, Lenny can't remember how many rooms he's checked into—providing a lucrative business for the motel.

So how does someone without short-term memory make his or her way in the world? How can I drive to work if I can't remember why I got in the car? How can I ever make new friends if I can't remember a face? How can I ever read a book if I forget the first chapter five minutes after reading it? In the face of these challenges, Leonard in his resourcefulness comes up with a "system"; others with Leonard's condition couldn't survive because they didn't have one. The system is simple: *writing*. Leonard's navigation through existence is governed by writing, by a collection of texts and notes—coupled with Polaroid photographs[3]—that substitute for memory. His pockets are filled with little texts, some written on napkins, others written on Polaroids, all providing the framework for him to understand his world. In his pocket is a snapshot of his Jaguar with the text "My Car" to remind him which vehicle in the parking lot belongs to him. All his acquaintances are noted in a similar way.

This system of texts and writing, however, works on the basis of two principles or beliefs: first, only trust your own handwriting; be suspicious of any writing you can't recognize. Second, really important information shouldn't be trusted to notes on napkins: vital information should be written on the body. Thus Leonard is himself a walking text, his body riddled with tattooed reminders: of historical events (like the murder of his wife), of basic principles (like "Consider the source" and "Memory is treachery"), and of "facts" about the case he is investigating, the murder of his wife (Leonard literally lives for revenge). Because his body is the source of so much knowledge, Leonard needs

2. Leonard repeatedly claims, "I know who I am; I know all about myself." In fact, this is far from the truth, as Teddy constantly reminds him: "You don't know who you are." He knows only who he *was*.

3. The visual images are ultimately subject to the word, since pictures without writing are useless for Lenny. He writes on the photos to remind himself of what or who they are. He needs the text to interpret the image.

to spend a lot of time in front of the mirror to remind himself about the reality of his world: what's history ("John G raped and murdered my wife"), what he's doing (seeking to avenge his wife), who he's looking for (an elusive "John G"), what the facts are, and what his basic beliefs are ("Learn by repetition," "Don't trust your weakness," "Camera doesn't lie," etc.). Leonard's entire relationship to the world is mediated by texts—some on his body, more scribbled on notes—all of which function as the framework through which he sees the world.

Without these texts, Leonard literally would not be able to have an experience of the world. Just having an experience requires a certain ability to integrate one's sensations over time. If I'm listening to a U2 song, in order for me to "get it," I need to be able to listen from beginning to end and then integrate what I've heard. Leonard's condition makes this impossible: by the end of the song, Lenny would have forgotten the beginning! The only way Leonard can keep his experience together—and hence have anything like a world of experience—is by a series of notes/texts that put together the world for him. Without texts, Leonard lacks a world. And without a pen, Leonard lacks a text. So when someone like Natalie wants to manipulate Leonard by transforming his world, all she has to do is put all the pens in her purse! When a disturbing event happens—one that Leonard wants to remember but Natalie would rather forget—the absence of any writing utensils means that the event is obliterated from Leonard's world.

Of course, this kind of system has its problems. As Natalie points out: "It must be tough living your life according to a couple of scraps of paper. Mix up your laundry list with your grocery list, and you'll end up eating your underwear for breakfast!" Living on texts in a world composed of notes entails both doubt and anxiety: how does Leonard know his texts really represent the world outside his mind? In fact, this is one of the nagging doubts that requires a constant faith and reassertion of belief on his part. One of Leonard's fundamental beliefs—though he has to keep reminding himself—is that there *is* a world outside his mind. As he confesses at the end of the film (which is the beginning of the story): "I have to believe in a world outside my own mind. I have to believe that my actions still have meaning, even if I can't remember it. I have to believe that when my eyes are closed, the world's still there. Do I believe . . . ?" Ultimately, the question he puts to himself is not whether the world exists outside his mind but whether he believes it.

Derrida's Claim: There Is Nothing outside the Text

According to many, Jacques Derrida is a kind of philosophical Leonard, or, conversely, *Memento* is a "deconstructive" film. "Deconstruction"—a term coined by Derrida in 1967—has entered even the most colloquial American vocabulary and is used to describe everything from architecture and music videos to key lime pie. Often it is used simply as a synonym for destruction or criticism; hence, to "deconstruct" something is to take it apart, to knock it down, to pull it apart piece by piece. But when Derrida introduced the term in the late 1960s, he did not intend it as a primarily negative notion, even if he did intend it as a kind of criticism. For Derrida deconstruction is ultimately positive and constructive. We'll return to this later.

What is the link between Leonard and Derrida, between *Memento* and deconstruction? It is the central role of texts or writing for mediating or putting together our experience of the world. For both Leonard and Derrida, language is the necessary filter through which the world comes to us. Just as Leonard depends on the writing of notes to give his world some coherence and order, so Derrida argues that all of us interpret our world on the basis of language (broadly understood). *Memento* ends with Leonard claiming that he's really no different than anyone else. In a way, that is the heart of Derrida's claim: like Lenny, we all need crib notes and cheat sheets to make our way in the world. In one of his first books, published in 1967 (in French), Derrida famously puts it this way: "There is nothing outside the text" [*Il n'y a pas de hors-texte*].[4]

Now, immediately, we need to consider the ways in which this claim has been misunderstood by the "bumper-sticker" approach. When someone—especially a philosopher—claims that there is nothing outside the text, it sounds as if he is claiming that the whole world is a kind of book—that there are no cups or tables

---

4. Jacques Derrida, *Of Grammatology*, trans. G. Spivak (Baltimore: Johns Hopkins University Press, 1976), 158; henceforth referred to in the text as *OG*.

or spouses. If there is nothing outside the text, then all we have are texts; and if all we have are texts, then we don't have things. In other words, Derrida sounds like a metaphysical idealist (like Berkeley) who claims that there are no material things, only ideas in the mind of God. As such, many have understood Derrida as a linguistic idealist who thinks there is only language, not things—only texts, not cups or tables. This is how he is commonly understood by Christians, especially Christian theologians.

Of course, a Christian could not be a linguistic idealist (someone who thinks there are only words, not things) for at least two reasons: First, if there is nothing outside the text, then a transcendent Creator who is distinct from and prior to the world could not exist. In this sense, linguistic idealism would have to entail atheism. If Derrida is a linguistic idealist, then deconstruction and Christian faith are mutually exclusive. Second, if there is nothing outside the text, then it would seem that what the Bible (admittedly a text) talks about—what it refers to—is not real. When the Bible speaks about the incarnation, or the effects of the work of Christ, or a spiritual warfare in the heavenly realms, all these references must not be real. But if these claims are not real—if it is not the case that Jesus really was God in the flesh (John 1:14), or if his death on the cross did not effect a cosmic transformation (Col. 1:20)—then Christianity is at best a fiction and at worst a waste of time. Thus the common conclusion is that Derrida's claim that there is nothing outside the text is antithetical to authentic Christian confession.

I suggest, however, that there is a problem with this conclusion. In particular, the conclusion rests on a faulty premise, namely, a serious misunderstanding of what Derrida means when he claims that there is nothing outside the text. The following discussion carefully considers the bigger picture surrounding Derrida's claim and suggests that, in fact, Derrida offers insight into the structure of creation.

Leonard's Condition as the Human Condition: Reading, Writing, and Interpretation

Derrida's provocative claim that there is nothing outside the text arises in the context of a discussion about reading and interpretation. Let us consider the passage in some detail in order to appreciate the nuances of what Derrida is saying. If we are going to do justice to postmodernism, our engagement with it needs to be characterized by charity—and charity requires time.

In *Of Grammatology*, the book in which Derrida makes this claim, he is engaged in an extended analysis of an essay by early modern thinker (and Genevan) Jean-Jacques Rousseau, "On the Origin of Language," which addresses a topic that deeply interests Derrida. In answering the question about the origins of language, Rousseau tends to think that language is an obstacle to the world, that language gets in the way of just experiencing the world itself. Language is a lens through which we see the world, albeit with some distortion, simply because this lens stands between us and the world. As soon as there is a lens, there is distortion. We can buff this lens for days or grind it as thin as possible, but this lens is mediation, and as soon as there is mediation, for Rousseau, there is distortion. Thus, Rousseau suggests that language is something that befalls us as a contingent evil, in a way corrupting what was a pure, unmediated experience of the world simply "as it is." Like Leonard in *Memento*, we have a condition (a disease, an illness) that requires us to use language to make our way in the world. Rousseau longs for the good old days (what he calls "the state of Nature") when we weren't afflicted with this condition and could simply experience the world the way it is without mediation—without anything between us and the world. In other words, for Rousseau, as soon as the lens of language is inserted, we have to interpret the world. As soon as there is mediation, there is interpretation. The "state of Nature" is a state of immediacy where we don't have to "interpret" things; we simply "know" what they are. That's a cup. That's my wife. This is a computer. It's clear and simple.[5] For Rousseau, Leonard—with his condition—is a freak, literally *un*-natural.

But was there ever a time without interpretation? Will there ever be a time when we don't interpret? Does one ever just simply see a cup "as it is"? Enter Derrida. Although Rousseau offered his theory in the sixteenth century—at the center of the birth of

---

5. I have analyzed the hermeneutics of immediacy in much more detail in the first chapter of my *Fall of Interpretation: Philosophical Foundations for a Creational Hermeneutic* (Downers Grove, IL: InterVarsity, 2000).

modernity—Derrida thinks that most of us twenty-first-century inhabitants are Rousseaueans at heart. This becomes most clear in our ideas of what it means to read.

Often when we read—and biblical commentaries tend to be a great case study for this—we imagine that the text or the language of the book is something we have to get *through* in order to recover the author's original intention. In other words, the text becomes a hurdle that we have to jump over—or a curtain we need to pass through—in order to get to what is behind the text, such as the author's idea or the referent (the thing to which the text points). Sometimes we concede that such a process requires that bothersome thing called interpretation—as when we're reading a poem or C. S. Lewis's more allegorical works. Then we concede that there is a kind of code that needs to be broken in order to understand the text. But most of the time, we don't think we interpret; we simply read. In these cases we assume that the text under consideration is clear and therefore doesn't require interpretation. We might need some background or context, but once those pieces are in place, we don't need to interpret. Instead, the text takes on a kind of transparency so that we can simply see what it means. So unlike Leonard, who needs notes and texts to help explain his world, we can move around without such supplements. When I read the newspaper, I don't need to "interpret"; I simply need to read. And most of us think that when we read the Bible, the same is true: yes, some passages are difficult, or the poetry of Song of Solomon might throw us for a loop, but if we're reading Paul's Epistle to the Romans, things are pretty clear. We simply need to provide a commentary that gives us the background and context. Such a commentary is like a cloth that cleans the text to grant it the transparency that makes interpretation unnecessary.

Derrida recognizes this kind of reading (he calls it "doubling commentary") and even concedes that there is a time and place for this kind of project. However, he worries that it assumes a kind of Rousseauean naiveté precisely because it assumes there can be a reading (or even experience) that does not involve interpretation. In other words, it assumes that we (who are either "normal," "healed," or "redeemed"—not beset by a "condition") are different from Leonard. Leonard is a freak; we are normal. Leonard needs notes and texts; we can simply look at the world

and see it "as it is." Even if we are reading a text, we can get past
it to what is behind it or the thing it is pointing to.

For Derrida, this is a naive assumption because it fails to recognize that we never really get "behind" or "past" texts; we never
get beyond the realm of interpretation to some kind of kingdom
of pure reading. We are never able to step out of our skins. Texts
and language are not something that we get through to a world
without language or a state of nature where interpretation is not
necessary. If the text is construed as an Alice-in-Wonderland-like
looking glass, on the other side is not a world without language or
interpretations but simply more texts and interpretation. Down
the rabbit hole of our experience, it is language all the way down.
Thus, just before making his famous claim that "there is nothing
outside the text," Derrida says that a reading or interpretation
"cannot legitimately transgress the text toward something other
than it, toward a referent . . . or toward a signified outside the text
whose content could take place, could have taken place outside
of language, that is to say, in the sense that we give here to that
word, outside of writing in general" (OG, 158). In other words,
if a line of text says, "The blue cup sat on Pilgrim's table," and I
understand what it means (I can picture a blue cup sitting on a
table), I have not, according to Derrida, stepped out of the realm
of interpretation. Interpretation is not a series of hoops we jump
through to eventually reach a realm of unmediated experience
where we don't have to interpret anymore. Rather, interpretation is an inescapable part of being human and experiencing the
world. So even this blue cup sitting on my table, from which I
am drinking my coffee "firsthand," as it were, is still a matter
of interpretation.

When Derrida says that we can't get beyond or behind the text
to a referent (or signified) that is outside language, he means this
in a radical way. There are a couple of less radical ways we could
understand this, which he notes but does not emphasize. First,
when he claims that there is nothing outside the text, this isn't
simply because "Jean-Jacques' life, or the existence of Mama or
Thérèse *themselves* is not of prime interest to us" (OG, 158). In
other words, he doesn't mean that we can just choose to act *as if*
Mama doesn't exist and play with the text without caring about
what it really refers to. That there is nothing outside the text is
not a voluntary condition that we can choose to effect. Second,

when he claims that there is nothing outside the text, this is not simply "because we have access to their so-called 'real' existence only in the text and we have neither any means of altering this, nor any right to neglect this limitation" (*OG*, 158). For instance, one might claim that there is no Socrates outside the text because the only access one has to Socrates is now through the texts of Plato or Aristophanes. In that sense there would be no Socrates outside the text.

While both these reasons would be sufficient grounds to proclaim that there is nothing outside the text, Derrida says "there are more radical reasons" (*OG*, 158). He goes on to note: "In what one calls the real life of these existences 'of flesh and bone,' beyond and behind what one believes can be circumscribed as Rousseau's text, there has never been anything but writing" (*OG*, 159). It is not just that writing or texts are the portal through which we must pass in order to get to things or the gates that provide access to an uninterpreted reality; rather, when Derrida claims that there is nothing outside the text, he means there is no reality that is not always already interpreted through the mediating lens of language.[6] Textuality, for Derrida, is linked to interpretation. To claim that there is nothing outside the text is to say that everything is a text, which means not that everything is a book, or that we live within a giant, all-encompassing book, but rather that everything must be interpreted in order to be experienced. Thus he is *not* a linguistic idealist who denies the material existence of cups and tables; rather, in the line of Martin Heidegger (of *Being and Time*), he is what we might call—for lack of a better term—a comprehensive hermeneuticist who asserts the ubiquity of interpretation: all our experience is always already an interpretation.

Texts that require interpretation are not things that are inserted between me and the world; rather, the world *is* a kind of text requiring interpretation. Even experiencing a cup "in

6. Thus, I concede that Leonard in *Memento* is not entirely a Derridean. Leonard still operates with a notion that there are facts that are not a matter of interpretation. Lenny thinks "memories are an interpretation" but that facts written on his body are not. But the film itself undermines Leonard's naive distinction, because one of the crucial facts that he writes down (the license number on Teddy's picture) is a pure fabrication just to give him someone to hunt down.

person" or "in the flesh" demands that I interpret the thing as a cup, and this interpretation is informed by a number of different things: the context in which I encounter the thing, my own history and background, the set of presuppositions that I bring to the experience, and more.[7] Given all these conditions, the things I experience are subject to interpretation—and as such, they are subject to *different* interpretations. Let's consider another example from film, not the heady world of *Memento* but the Disney world of *The Little Mermaid*. While I think the main character, Ariel, is corrupted by a consumerist desire, I'll bracket my extended social critique of the movie and here consider just one scene that illustrates the point that our firsthand experience of things themselves requires interpretation.

Ariel, though she is the daughter of King Triton and has all of the undersea world at her fingertips, still wants more. Indeed, the anthem of the film is her *cri de coeur* in which she expresses her heartfelt desire for more—to be part of the human world. Still confined to life under the ocean's surface, every once in a while Ariel ascends to the surface, where she has befriended Scuttle, a seagull who, obviously, lives above the sea and has contact with the human world of sailors and landlubbers. Scuttle is thus a mediator between the undersea world of Ariel and the human culture she desires to join. One of the ways she harbors this desire for human culture is by collecting artifacts from the human world and storing them in a kind of *Wunderzimmer*, or "room of wonders," her own undersea museum of humanity. Scuttle is one of her primary resources, not only acquiring the items for her but also naming and explaining them. When he gives her what we recognize as a smoking pipe, Scuttle tells Ariel it is a "snorflap," which is used for making music (and bubbles) by blowing into the mouthpiece. When he adds a fork to her collection, he names it a "dinglehopper" and explains that it is used for styling one's hair, like a comb or a brush. Each of the items in Ariel's collection—and her understanding of what they are—is situated by Scuttle's explanation.

7. I have analyzed the process and conditions of interpretation in much more detail in my *Fall of Interpretation*, especially chapter 5 (chapter 4 focuses on Derrida).

Through a number of machinations, Ariel finally gets a chance to make a foray into the human world. In particular, she is afforded the opportunity to try to win the love of a prince with whom she has been infatuated ever since she glimpsed him during one of her trips to the surface. One of the prices for her adventure into human culture was selling her melodious voice to an evil witch. So when she encounters the prince, she can't talk or explain herself. Although mute, Ariel is nonetheless charming and beautiful, and the prince invites her to join him for dinner at his castle. Ariel excitedly accepts and, before we know it, is seated at the prince's table—a site for communion with this human world. This world, of course, is not her own, and she has difficulty navigating her way through the experience (on top of learning to walk). So when she is seated to dine and finally recognizes something familiar in this strange world, she is eager to demonstrate her facility with this cultural artifact. What does she spy there but—can it be?—a *dinglehopper*! Immediately she seizes the item and begins brushing her hair with the flair of a longtime user. The prince, as you can imagine, is puzzled by such a strange employment of a fork!

This thing—this strangely shaped piece of metal—even when we find it sitting on the table right in front of us, is subject to interpretation. Given our horizons of experience, our past history, what we've been told, and thus a whole host of presuppositions that we bring to the experience, we immediately see the object as a fork (and find it difficult to really see it as anything *but* a fork).[8] But for Ariel—with her different history, different experience, and thus different presuppositions—the item is

8. Because children's horizons are fluid and unsedimented, they are able to see the world in ways that adults do not: a pair of underpants can be construed as a space helmet, or for just about every boy (in North American culture, that is), any object is susceptible to being seen as a gun. As we gain experience, our horizons and presuppositions begin to solidify; as a result, our seeing becomes more quickly determined and habitual. But at the same time, it seems that we become less open to seeing differently. Much of twentieth-century art (e.g., Picasso) worked at trying to make our horizons of expectation fluid once again, inviting us to see differently, "with the eyes of a child," as it were. Thus Picasso once remarked that the key to his work was unlearning what he had learned as an adult and recovering the way he saw the world as a child (see E. H. Gombrich, *The Story of Art*, 16th ed. [London: Phaidon, 1995], 573, 575). Given that we are invited to have faith "as a child," perhaps that entails keeping our horizons of

interpreted as a dinglehopper. While it might seem as though we don't even interpret the object, we actually go through the interpretive process so quickly, without even thinking about it, that it seems as if we're not engaged in interpretation. But the speed with which the object is construed as a fork does not negate the fact of interpretation or the interpretive process involved. So we never get past texts and interpretations to things "simply as they are" in any kind of unmediated fashion (as Rousseau supposed); rather, we move from interpretation to interpretation. All the world is a text. Thus, "there is nothing outside the text."

Derrida does not deny that the material phenomena we bump into—like forks and cups—have existence outside books and our minds. As he has repeatedly emphasized, he is not advocating a kind of linguistic idealism.[9] As such, the earlier criticisms of Derrida by Christian thinkers miss the mark. But does this mean there is nothing about Derrida's claim that might make Christians nervous? With an eye to appreciating the implications of Derrida's claim, we could loosely translate "There is nothing outside the text" simply with the axiom "Everything is interpretation." Or, in other words, "It is interpretation all the way down." For many Christians, this isn't much of an improvement. For some reason, at this point many Christians become nervous and assume that the claim that "everything is interpretation" is antithetical to Christian faith. Even if we understand Derrida's claim not as linguistic idealism but rather as ubiquitous interpretation, it would seem that we have a third reason why Derrida's claim is antithetic to Christian faith. If everything is interpretation, then even the gospel is only an interpretation and not objectively true.

---

expectation fluid rather than sedimented so that we are open to seeing God's miraculous work in the world.

9. Derrida later emphasizes that "there is nothing outside the text" does "not mean that all referents are suspended, denied, or enclosed in a book, as people have claimed, or have been naïve enough to believe and to have accused [me] of believing" (afterword to *Limited Inc*, trans. Samuel Weber [Evanston: Northwestern University Press, 1988], 148). For further discussion, see my "Limited Inc/arnation: The Searle/Derrida Debate Revisited in Christian Context," in *Hermeneutics at the Crossroads: Interpretation in Christian Perspective*, ed. Kevin Vanhoozer, James K. A. Smith, and Bruce Ellis Benson (Bloomington: Indiana University Press, forthcoming).

Derrida at the Foot of the Cross

Let's consider this criticism of Derrida more carefully. If the claim that there is nothing outside the text means that everything is interpretation, then the gospel would be only an interpretation. If it is only an interpretation, then that means there might be other interpretations. And if the gospel is only an interpretation and there could be other interpretations, we can't know if the gospel is true. A version of this criticism can be found in D. A. Carson's criticisms of the emerging church. Carson is clearly worried that because folks like Stanley Grenz, Brian McLaren, and other "hard postmodernists" (as he calls them) reject modern notions of absolute or "objective" truth, they are giving up on truth altogether. But in his criticisms, it becomes clear that Carson simply conflates truth with objectivity: for Carson, one can only be said to know "truly" if one knows "objectively."[10] While Carson rightly notes that human knowledge can never pretend to omniscience, this doesn't mean we can't claim to know in a finite but real manner. But his affirmation of finite knowledge always elides into an affirmation of objective knowledge. Although he does not define objectivity (quite an oversight, given his project), Carson clearly means this to carry some connotation of self-evident givenness: if a truth is objective, then it is not a matter of interpretation. Thus, if Derrida is not a linguistic idealist but nevertheless asserts that everything is interpretation, then according to folks like Carson, such a claim is antithetical to the (supposedly biblical!) requirement that what is true be objective. If the gospel is an interpretation, and therefore not "objective," then it would seem that it cannot be true.

10. See D. A. Carson, *Becoming Conversant with the Emerging Church: Understanding a Movement and Its Implications* (Grand Rapids: Zondervan, 2005), 105, 130–31, 143n46. The simplicity of this unwarranted conflation then underwrites the long concordance of passages he lists in chapter 7 (188–200), which he takes to be clear evidence that the Bible, because it speaks of "truth" and "knowing," therefore also advocates the modern epistemological notion of objectivity. As he puts it, "objective truth" is a "category . . . that both historic Christianity and the Bible itself have always insisted on" (126)! But this simply is not the case; in fact, as we will see below, the Scriptures give us good reasons to reject the very notion of objectivity, while at the same time affirming the reality of truth and knowledge.

Again, allow me to put this into slow motion in order to do justice to the issues. On the one hand, this criticism is right. I would agree that the gospel is an interpretation and that we can't *know* the gospel is true, *if* by knowledge we mean unmediated objectivity or pure access to "the way things are" (a Rousseauean dream).[11] On the other hand, it is wrong to conclude that this is antithetical to orthodox Christian faith. This third kind of criticism is loaded with unjustified assumptions about the nature of interpretation and the question of truth because it assumes that if something is an interpretation, it can't be true; or, conversely, it assumes that if something is true, it must be objective. As such, it harbors something of the Rousseauean notion that assumes interpretation is a disease—like Leonard's condition—that pollutes and corrupts our relationship to the world. But the fact that something is a matter of interpretation does not mean that an interpretation cannot be true or a good interpretation. When I construe this thing in front of me as a cup and use it to drink my coffee, although I am interpreting the cup, I am also interpreting it *well*. True, the cup does not exist as some brute fact, but that doesn't mean that my interpreted understanding of the cup is not good or true.

Let's get right to the heart of the matter by means of a thought experiment. Our central question here is whether Derrida's (paraphrased) claim that everything is interpretation is antithetical to orthodox Christian faith. I suggest that it is not. To do so, imagine with me two inhabitants of Jerusalem in the early first century. Here is their account of a particular day's event, not unfamiliar to us:

> It was the Passover, and like most others—both natives and visitors for the feast—we'd heard about the events transpiring, first in the governor's palace and then just outside the city on Golgotha. So out of curiosity—we're too busy for silliness like religion—we

---

11. Here I agree with Carson that we should reject a common postmodern move that equates knowledge with omniscience, and then, since it is clear that such is not possible for finite beings, we must end up as skeptics with respect to knowledge (see ibid., 104–7). Such versions of postmodernism still adhere to the Cartesian criterion for knowledge; they just consider it impossible. We will consider the question of objectivity further in chapter 3, when we discuss why Christianity is not a metanarrative.

made our way outside the city gates to catch a glimpse of the spectacle [CNN not yet being there to deceive them into thinking they've seen events unfold from the comfort of their living rooms]. There was a great deal of commotion—more than usual for Passover. Around Golgotha we heard both sneers and weeping, some people taunting and others sobbing. We were there to see some of the Roman guard gambling for a few scraps of clothes (Matt. 27:35), as well as some of the religious authorities gloating over their power. The center of attention, of course, was the crosses on this clump of a hill—particularly the one in the center, where a Nazarene hung. We've said it for years: What good can come out of Nazareth! Nazarenes end up as either servants, prisoners, or unfortunates punished for capital crimes. This one just confirmed the point again. On the central cross where this Nazarene was hanging—pathetic and beaten—a sign was posted proclaiming that he was "King of the Jews" (with something written in other languages, too, but we didn't know what they said). Are all these women crying because they actually believed that? we wondered. We're not sure who was more pathetic: the one hanging there on the tree or those who had put their hope in a Nazarene. King of the Jews. What is this? A joke? Judging from the smug laughter of the chief priests, that must be it.

After lunch, things did get a little strange: it was dark until about three o'clock in the afternoon—but authorities later reported it had been a solar eclipse. As the light began to return, the pathetic Nazarene started blurting out something about Elijah—but in doing so he seemed to expend his last gasp of energy and hung lifeless on the cross. Another cross, another Nazarene, another criminal—one less to worry about. The coincidence of an earth tremor at the same moment contributed to the commotion, but soon enough the crowds began to disperse. Sure, the women remained there weeping, still clinging to their naive hope that a Nazarene could be some kind of king—but we had been cured of such illusions long ago. So, like most of the other curiosity seekers, we joined the caravan heading back into the city, hoping to find some supper left at home.

Now consider an alternative account, that of a centurion posted as a guard on Golgotha that same afternoon (cf. Matt. 27:54):

I'm not sure why my number was called, except for experience and a certain acquaintance with the events leading up to that day.

My responsibility—along with the rest of my cohort—was to keep surveillance at the scene of a crucifixion just outside Jerusalem. In many ways, this was like a hundred other crucifixions I had witnessed, but with a special, almost laughable twist: that day we would execute a Nazarene—a Nazarene!—who had claimed to be a king, "the King of the Jews." Everyone, both we Romans as well as Jerusalem's own religious leaders, got the joke, so the sign that we posted on the Nazarene's cross was intended just as a way of letting others in on it.

The background experience that familiarized me with the situation was somewhat secondhand. An old friend, Antony—a fellow with whom I'd gone through the academy—at one time had a direct encounter with this Nazarene [cf. Matt. 8:5–13]. When he was stationed just outside Capernaum, not far from Nazareth, news and rumors of the healings performed by a Jesus—a carpenter from Nazareth—often circulated throughout the area. Antony's servant, who had ministered to Antony in his own illness, was lying paralyzed at home, writhing in agony from a pain that Antony couldn't see and an illness that Roman doctors could not diagnose. In the throes of both desperation and what must have been madness, Antony made his way to Capernaum to make one last effort on behalf of his suffering servant. As Antony later recounted the story to me, what appeared mad desperation when he left his house took on both hope and a kind of reasonableness when he found himself near this Jesus. Though he had left his house with slim hope and vast doubts, in the presence of this Nazarene he found himself energized by deep faith and great hope. With a confidence that almost startled him, Antony told this Jesus: "Just say the word, and I know that my servant will be healed." By the time Antony reached home, his servant was already fixing dinner! But Antony wasn't surprised.

Not having been there, though being infected somewhat by the elation in Antony's narration, I found it easy in the months that followed to either forget the story or discount it. True, there was a certain irony when I was later given the assignment of overseeing the Nazarene's crucifixion, but life is full of such funny coincidences. A couple of times Antony's tale slipped out from the caverns of my memory into consciousness, but for the most part this was just another criminal, just another Nazarene. Another day, another crucifixion.

Of course, this particular crucifixion was unlike others: the chief priests and religious leaders weren't usually milling about outside the city gates like this. And they usually didn't take such delight in the crucifixion of a Jew. And while we could usually expect to find the mothers of criminals wailing at the foot of the cross, the cohort of women weeping for this Jesus was certainly out of the ordinary. And aside from continuing to protest their innocence and casting insults at those of us just doing our jobs, these defeated beings hanging on the cross usually didn't say much. And they certainly didn't say the kind of things this Jesus said.

At first I found it pitiable and a bit irritating, listening to this Nazarene making these pronouncements. But admittedly, I'd never heard a crucified one pray for us to be forgiven or promise other criminals that they would join him in paradise. While others in our cohort mocked and gambled for his clothes, slapping the backs of the chief priests, who usually detested them, I found myself retreating from the experience, as it were—finding myself a foreigner in a strange land, going through the motions of my job but with Antony's story ringing in my ear, reverberating with what the Nazarene himself had just said: "It is finished."

After that, things became eerie as the sky darkened for three hours. We had to remain on guard, not sure what was happening, but the darkness seemed to discourage not only commotion but even speech. And so there I found myself, in the dark, effectually alone (though surrounded by hundreds), with a strange silence echoing in such a way that it seemed to be asking me a question: "Who is this man?" I can't replay for you the turmoil of that questioning. I can simply witness to this: when the darkness lifted, and an earthquake seemed to shake the very foundations of the earth itself, those for me were but tiny cosmic ripples of a dawning within my own life and a shaking of my own foundations. For at that point, after wrestling with God for over three hours—struggling with the testimonies of Antony and my own experience on Golgotha—I could finally articulate an answer to my question: "Truly this was the Son of God!"

These two extended accounts of a series of events illustrate the way in which the gospel itself is an interpretation, helping us to appreciate Derrida's claim—and why Derrida's claim is not antithetical to Christian faith. Each of these accounts is an interpretation of events in first-century Jerusalem. Each of them is a response to Jesus of Nazareth. Each of them is a "reading" of what took place and the phenomena in front of each narrator. Each is a kind of textual rendering of what happened. But, of course, the renderings and interpretations are very different. If we, as

Christians, agree with the interpretation of the centurion—and with him confess that this is the true account of what took place on that afternoon—our agreement does not mitigate the fact that this is an interpretation. If we appeal to God's special revelation about these events attested in the Scriptures, this does not change the fact that it remains an interpretation of what took place. In fact, the appeal to revelation only strengthens the claim that the centurion's reading is an interpretation: without that revelation we might be in the situation of the two natives of Jerusalem: all we see is another cross, another Nazarene.

Revelation informs our horizon. However, even the (objective) provision of a revelatory interpretation does not guarantee that everyone will read the event in this way. One must (subjectively) accept this revelatory interpretation, which requires faith—and such faith requires the regenerating work of the Holy Spirit. Again, see Owen's discussion in *The Holy Spirit* (repr., Grand Rapids: Kregel, 1954). As he puts it, God's provision of objective light (revelation) does not resolve the problem of subjective darkness (148ff.). In other words, the objective provision of revelation in the Scriptures is ineffectual as revelation (i.e., to communicate) without the regeneration of the heart and mind in order to dispel blindness.

Christians who become skittish about the claim that everything is interpretation are usually hanging on to a very modern notion of knowledge, one that claims something is true only insofar as it is objective—insofar as it can be universally known by all people, at all times, in all places. On this account, the truth of the gospel—that God was in Christ reconciling the world to himself—is taken to be objectively true and thus capable of rational demonstration. (Classical apologetics buys this epistemology, or theory of knowledge.) If we say that the gospel is an interpretation, then it is not objectively true in the traditional or modern sense of being self-evident or universally demonstrable.[12]

The problem with this very modern construal of the gospel is that it doesn't match up with the witness of the New Testament. It is clear from the Gospel narratives, for instance, that

12. For a helpful discussion of this point, see Philip Kenneson's "There's No Such Thing as Objective Truth, and It's a Good Thing, Too," in *Christian Apologetics in a Postmodern World*, ed. Timothy R. Phillips and Dennis Okholm (Downers Grove, IL: InterVarsity, 1995), 155–70.

not everyone sees what the centurion sees. Of course, they all see and encounter the same material realities—crosses, bodies, and eventually corpses—but these material phenomena are texts that need to be interpreted. Thus the very fact that both the centurion and the chief priests are confronted by the same phenomena and yet see something very different seems to demonstrate Derrida's point: the very experience of the things themselves is a matter of interpretation. Even if we are confronted with the physical and historical evidence of the resurrection—even if we witnessed the resurrection firsthand—what exactly this meant would require interpretation. Only by interpreting the resurrection of Jesus does one see that it confirms that he is the Son of God (Rom. 1:4). As John Owen observes: "That Jesus Christ was crucified, is a proposition that any natural [i.e., unregenerate] man may understand and assent to, and be said to receive: and all the doctrines of the gospel may be taught in propositions and discourses, the sense and meaning of which a natural man may understand; but it is denied that he can receive the things themselves. For there is a wide difference between the mind's receiving doctrines notionally, and receiving the things taught in them really."[13]

Moreover, in the epistles we get the same kind of claim, namely, that not everyone can see what the believer sees. While God's invisible attributes are, on the one hand, "clearly seen" (Rom. 1:20), Paul goes on to emphasize the way in which this is not seen by those whose "foolish hearts were darkened" (1:21), who thus construe or interpret the world as something other than God's creation. While I agree that interpreting the world as creation is the true interpretation, this does not negate its status as an interpretation. What is required to interpret the world well is the necessary conditions of interpretation—the right horizons of expectation and the right presuppositions. But as Paul repeatedly emphasizes, these conditions are themselves a gift; in other words, the presuppositions and horizons that make it possible to properly "read" creation are grace gifts that attend redemption and regeneration (Rom. 1:18–31; 1 Cor. 1:18–2:15; Eph. 4:17–18). This is precisely why we shouldn't be surprised that not everyone we encounter immediately grasps the rationality of the gospel. In

13. Owen, *Holy Spirit*, 155.

fact, we should expect that someone will not be able to properly "see" creation or the crucifixion without the grace of redemption. Or, to put it another way, presuppositional apologetics—such as that developed by Francis Schaeffer, but also by Cornelius Van Til and, to a degree, Herman Dooyeweerd—rejects classical apologetics precisely because presuppositionalism recognizes the truth of Derrida's claim that everything is interpretation (though I am admittedly radicalizing their intuitions).

To embrace this (creational!) reality of ubiquitous interpretation requires that we embrace the corresponding reality of pluralism. Wherever there is interpretation, there will be conflict of interpretation or at least differences of interpretation. However, it is important to consider two levels, or modes, of this hermeneutic pluralism. On the one hand, a kind of pluralism and interpretive difference is inscribed into the very fabric of created finitude, such that we all see the same things but from different angles and locations. We all bump into the same stuff; it's just that some see it as a dinglehopper, others as a fork. In both Eden and the eschaton, we find interpretive pluralism that is rooted in this plurality of perspectives. As a factor of the conditions of a good creation, this kind of pluralism is something we must embrace as good (Gen. 1:31).[14] And such interpretive pluralism remains a reality within the church. On the other hand, a kind of deep "directional"[15] pluralism is endemic to our postlapsarian (post-fall) condition; that is, there is a level of interpretive difference that concerns fundamental issues such as what it means to be authentically human and how we fit into the cosmos. In this respect, for instance, Christianity and Buddhism have very different interpretations about the nature of reality. However, we need to consider these as deep differences in interpretation rather than glibly supposing that the Christian account is objectively true and then castigating the Buddhist account for being merely an interpretation. In fact, both are interpretations; neither is *objectively* true. And so, to a certain extent, we must also embrace this postlapsarian or directional pluralism as the given situation

14. I have explained this in more detail in *The Fall of Interpretation*, chapter 5.

15. I am drawing here on a suggestive and underappreciated analysis of pluralism in Richard Mouw and Sander Griffioen, *Pluralisms and Horizons: An Essay in Christian Public Philosophy* (Grand Rapids: Eerdmans, 1993).

in which we find ourselves. To assert that our interpretation is not an interpretation but objectively true often translates into the worst kinds of imperial and colonial agendas, even within a pluralist culture. Acknowledging the interpreted status of the gospel should translate into a certain humility in our public theology. It should not, however, translate into skepticism about the truth of the Christian confession. If the interpretive status of the gospel rattles our confidence in its truth, this indicates that we remain haunted by the modern desire for objective certainty. But our confidence rests not on objectivity but rather on the convictional power of the Holy Spirit (which isn't exactly objective); the loss of objectivity, then, does not entail a loss of kerygmatic boldness about the truth of the gospel.

Deconstruction's recognition that everything is interpretation opens a space of questioning—a space to call into question the received and dominant interpretations that often claim not to be interpretations at all. As such, deconstruction is interested in interpretations that have been marginalized and sidelined, activating voices that have been silenced. This is the constructive, yea prophetic, aspect of Derrida's deconstruction: a concern for justice by being concerned about dominant, status quo interpretations that silence those who see differently. Thus, from its inception, deconstruction has been, at root, ethical—concerned for the paradigmatic marginalized described by the Old Testament as "the widow, the orphan, and the stranger." To put it differently: Wall Street and Washington both want us to think that their rendering of the world is "just the way things are." Deconstruction, by showing the way in which everything is interpretation, empowers us to question the interpretations of trigger-happy presidents and greedy CEOs—in a way not unlike the prophets' questioning of the dominant interpretations of the world. As such, we are free to interpret the world differently. When we reflect on the implications of deconstruction for the church later, we'll consider this prophetic conclusion of deconstruction's claim in more detail.

Texts in Community

Derrida's claim that there is nothing outside the text was often misunderstood, and not just by Christian theologians. Later, when presented with the opportunity, Derrida tried to clarify his claim: "The phrase that for some has become a sort of slogan of deconstruction, in general so badly understood ('there is nothing outside the text'), means nothing other than: *there is nothing outside context*."[16] In a way, Derrida is repeating the axiom of real estate as a central condition of interpretation: location, location, location! The context of both the phenomenon (whether a book, a cup, or an event) and the interpreter function as conditions or frameworks that determine just how a thing is seen or understood. Just as he claims that there is nothing outside the text, elsewhere Derrida claims that "there are only contexts."[17] Context, then, determines the meaning of a text, the construal of a thing, or the "reading" of an event. For instance, part of the context of the centurion's "reading" of the crucifixion was his compatriot's earlier experience with the gentle healer from Nazareth—a context that the two natives of Jerusalem lacked. (I would also argue that grace formed part of the centurion's context.)

When Derrida talks about how contexts are "determined" or "filled in," we find a very important (though largely ignored) emphasis in his work: the role of community in interpretation. As he explains in his afterword to *Limited Inc*, contexts are flexible and dynamic: contexts change as time and place changes, generating different meanings and interpretations. Derrida describes this as the possibility of *recontextualization*: a phrase can mean one thing in one context and something different in another—just as the metal item is a fork in one context and a dinglehopper in another. Contexts change, and therefore meanings are given to change: if I shout "Duck!" in a field while we're hunting, you will look upward for a target; if we're golfing and I shout "Duck!" you should assume a fetal position to avoid an incoming projectile. The same word, *duck*, is recontextualized. And insofar as a context can never be completely "filled in," any text, thing, or event is susceptible to different construals and interpretations. Because Derrida has emphasized this play and

16. Derrida, afterword to *Limited Inc*, 136, emphasis added, translation modified.
17. Jacques Derrida, "Signature Event Context," in *Margins of Philosophy*, trans. Alan Bass (Chicago: University of Chicago Press, 1982), 320. For a more detailed discussion of this point, see my "Limited Inc/arnation."

flexibility of contexts, many have concluded that he thinks we can just interpret things any way we want—that texts and events can be played with and we can simply make up the meaning as we go. For instance, they think Derrida's claim means that you can make the Bible say anything you want.

Of course, on the one hand, this is completely true—and once again, if we look at our experience, we see that Derrida is right: people and groups do interpret the Bible in all kinds of ways, and they do make the Bible say whatever they want it to say. We all know the truism that you can prove just about anything by quoting from the Bible, whether it be a justification of slavery or why Christians shouldn't have mortgages. Obviously, the Bible is subject to all kinds of interpretations. But this play of interpretations does not mean that all these interpretations are good or true. Deconstruction does not entail that one can say just anything at all about a text; it is not a celebration of sheer indeterminacy. "Otherwise," Derrida protests, "one could indeed say just anything at all and I have never accepted saying, or encouraging others to say, just anything at all."[18] Instead, Derrida emphasizes that there are important, legitimate determinations of context; in particular, the context for understanding a text, thing, or event is established by a community of interpreters who come to an agreement about what constitutes the true interpretation of a text, thing, or event. Given the goals and purpose of a given community, it establishes a consensus regarding the rules that will govern good interpretation. So, within the human community, the metal object with pointy ends is to be understood as a fork and employed as an eating utensil, not as a comb. Although the object is susceptible to interpretation as a comb, such a construal is ruled a bad interpretation by the community. Without the rules established by a community, there would be no criteria to govern interpretation. And Derrida is not opposed to rules as such. In fact, he speaks positively about a community having a kind of "interpretive police" to govern interpretation for that community.[19] Thus communities fix contexts, and contexts determine meanings. This role of community will become central as we think about what it means to interpret the Scriptures.

18. Derrida, afterword to *Limited Inc*, 144–45.
19. Ibid., 131, 146.

Taking Derrida to Church

We've now come quite a way from the bumper-sticker misunderstandings of Derrida to a clearer understanding of Derrida's claim that there is nothing outside the text. As we've seen, he means roughly that everything is interpretation; interpretation is governed by context and the role of the interpretive community. This entails abandoning the modern notion of objectivity and embracing a central theme of postmodernism: interpretation goes "all the way down."

But we still haven't fully answered our third objector, who suggested that if interpretation goes all the way down, then the gospel can't be known to be true. We've begun to answer that objection by showing the way in which the gospel must be an interpretation. But what are the implications of accepting Derrida's claim that there is nothing outside the text? What would that mean for our understanding of the gospel, Scripture, and church?

Seeing the World through the Word

Derrida has suggested that all the world is a text. As a text, it is subject to interpretation, and interpretation brings in the role of our horizons of perception and our presuppositions. These horizons or presuppositions are informed by our fundamental beliefs about the world as well as our past experiences and encounters with the world. There is no uninterpreted reality, no brute facts passively sitting there to be simply and purely seen. Rather, we see the world always already through the lens of an interpretive framework governed by ultimate beliefs. We could say that we always already see the world through a worldview. And part of Derrida's claim, much like the claim of presuppositional apologists like Schaeffer and Van Til, is that this is the case for everyone.[20] We all—whether naturalists, atheists, Buddhists, or Christians—see the world through the grid of an interpretive framework—and ultimately this interpretive framework is reli-

---

20. This claim should be compared to Thomas Kuhn's analysis of the paradigms that govern scientific observation of the world in his landmark book *The Structure of Scientific Revolutions*, 2nd ed. (Chicago: University of Chicago Press, 1970). I have discussed this in my *Fall of Interpretation*, 154–55.

gious in nature, even if not allied with a particular institutional religion.[21]

This insight should help us appreciate two things: First, if one of the crucial insights of postmodernism is that everyone comes to his or her experience of the world with a set of ultimate presuppositions, then Christians should not be afraid to lay their specifically Christian presuppositions on the table and allow their account to be tested in the marketplace of ideas (we'll talk more about this in chapter 2). In a way, Derrida has brought the broader culture to appreciate what Christian thinkers like Abraham Kuyper, Herman Dooyeweerd, Cornelius Van Til, and Francis Schaeffer have been saying for a long time: that our ultimately religious presuppositions govern our understanding of the world. Second, and more constructively, this should push us to ask ourselves whether the biblical text is what truly governs our seeing of the world. If all the world is a text to be interpreted, then for the church the narrative of the Scriptures is what should govern our very perception of the world. We should see the world through the Word. In this sense, then, Derrida's claim could be resonant with the Reformers claim of *sola scriptura*, which simply emphasizes the priority of God's special revelation for our understanding of the world and making our way in it. There is nothing outside the Text, we might say. And to say that there is nothing outside the Text, then, is to emphasize that there is not a single square inch of our experience of the world that should not be governed by the revelation of God in the Scriptures. To say that there is nothing outside the Text is to say that there is no aspect of creation to which God's revelation does not speak. But do we really let the Text govern our seeing of the world? Or have we become more captivated by the stories and texts of a consumerist culture? Is our worldview shaped by the narratives of a hip-hop culture more than the stories of God's covenantal relationship with his people? One of the challenges of Christian discipleship is to make the text of the Scripture the Text outside which nothing stands. As U2's song "When You Look at the World" attests, this is not always

21. On this final point, see Roy A. Clouser, *The Myth of Religious Neutrality: An Essay on the Hidden Role of Religious Belief in Theories*, rev. ed. (Notre Dame: Notre Dame University Press, 2005); and idem., *Knowing with the Heart: Religious Experience and Belief in God* (Downers Grove, IL: InterVarsity, 1999).

easy; sometimes I "can't see what You see, when I look at the world." But the sanctification of the Spirit is aimed at enabling us to see the world through this lens.

Interpreting as if We Believe the Apostles' Creed

In many ways, modernity is characterized by a deep individualism that isolates us from one another, sealed up in our little egos or private spheres. It is not unimportant that Descartes' *Meditations*—in many ways a manifesto of modernity—was the result of Descartes shutting himself up in his room alone for a number of days just to think by himself. This modern isolationist understanding of the human self has often crept into the church, which has too often valorized a notion of private interpretation (by wrongly appealing to the Reformation principle of the perspicuity of Scripture), suggesting that the meaning of the Scriptures is simply and objectively there—available for the taking.

Such an individualistic notion, however, has nothing to do with the Reformers, let alone the ancient church. As we confess in the Apostles' Creed, we believe in both "the holy, catholic church" and "the communion of the saints." And Derrida's critique of modernity, along with his emphasis on community, helps us appreciate the way in which postmodernity pushes us to recapture the central role of community not only for biblical interpretation but also for teaching us how to make our way in the world. One of the things that Leonard lacks in the film *Memento* is a community of friends he can trust. (In fact, one of his rules—tattooed on his body—is to trust no one.) But as Derrida demonstrates, we can't interpret a text, thing, or event without the conventions and rules of an interpretive community; indeed, language itself is inherently communal and intersubjective. (And eventually even Leonard has to trust someone else, as when he trusts the note written in Natalie's handwriting.) For instance, to interpret the Scriptures, and interpret them *well*, I cannot shut myself off from the community that is the church; rather, I need to be formed and informed by the breadth of this community, both geographically (the global church) and temporally (history of the church's witness). While the church is governed by the Scriptures, the Scriptures are only properly opened and active within the believing community. To say that there is nothing outside the Text also entails that there is no proper understanding of the Text—and hence the world—apart from the Spirit-governed community of the church. The same Spirit is both author of the text and illuminator of the reading community.

A Deconstructive Church

If, as I have claimed, Derrida has something to say to the contemporary church, what would a deconstructive church look like? Here I would like to offer a tour of a church that has engaged Derrida and see what it might look like in action.

First, one is struck by the difference between a deconstructive church that affirms there is nothing outside the Text and the kind of postmodern church sketched by others. As we participate in the worship of a deconstructive church, we find that the Text is central for shaping our interpretation of the world. In order to take the totality of the text seriously, the deconstructive church employs the revered tradition of the lectionary, which, over the course of a few years, guides us through the entirety of the Text's narrative, rather than leaving us to the private canons and pet texts of the pastor. This use of the lectionary is part of a general impression that tradition is valued in the deconstructive church. We recite the ecumenical and historic creeds because these are the witness of our community past—the way for us to hear the interpretations of the ancient community, which was indwelt by the same Spirit that indwells us and grants illumination today. The pastor's preaching indicates a serious engagement with the early fathers and the Reformers as co-interpreters. All of this helps us understand that the church is a community, a "holy, catholic church," which has endured through millennia.

The voices of the community are not only ancient, however; they are also global. The singing and prayers are drawn from Christian communities in southern France and South Korea, from Scotland and Zimbabwe. These other voices—so often marginalized by the Western church—are received as voices of the Spirit at work in our global brothers and sisters, illuminating us by illuminating them. Thus the deconstructive church, while having a sense of being traditional, is nevertheless characterized by a diversity and global concern that disrupts the status quo. The deconstructive church embraces tradition but not the tradition-alism of the status quo. It is a community of interpretation that values marginalized readings—largely because the "foolishness" of the gospel itself is an interpretation of the human condition sidelined by secular modernity. To proclaim the gospel is actually already to speak from the margins.

Finally, we note that this church, while recognizing that the gospel is an interpretation of the world and the human condition—perhaps *because* it recognizes this is an interpretation—focuses on the proclamation and witness of revelation. It does not focus on an apologetics of demonstration or on a "culture wars" agenda that, using logic as a weapon, seems to think that all Americans should simply see that Christianity is true. In fact, we can't help but be impressed by the prophetic stance of the deconstructive church with respect to its culture. One of the primary goals of the worship experience—embracing Word, sacrament, prayer, and singing—is to equip and empower the saints to see through the interpretations of the world and the human prospect offered by the cultural forces of capitalism, consumerism, and hedonism. In other words, the worship in a deconstructive church is aimed at forming believers who can recognize Wall Street's construal of happiness *as* an interpretation as well as articulate the countercultural gospel's interpretation of human flourishing. The deconstructive church, in other words, is deeply prophetic—reflecting the voice not so much of Derrida as of Amos.

3

Where Have All the Metanarratives Gone?

Lyotard, Postmodernism, and the Christian Story

Perhaps no definition of postmodernity has seemed so opposed to Christian faith as Jean-François Lyotard's claim that postmodernism is "incredulity toward metanarratives." Isn't the Bible a metanarrative par excellence? Wouldn't being postmodern, then, require rejecting the Bible? That question is the central focus of this chapter.

Raising the Curtain: *O Brother, Where Art Thou?*

We never tire of stories, especially grand epic tales of adventure and adversity. The Coen brothers' film *O Brother, Where Art Thou?*[1] tells just such a grand story, replaying another epic—Homer's *Odyssey*—in the context of Depression-era Mississippi.

1. *O Brother, Where Art Thou?* DVD, directed by Joel and Ethan Coen (Burbank, CA: Touchstone Home Video, 2001).

Like Homer's narrative, this story stars a Ulysses: the scheming and loquacious Ulysses Everett McGill, who goes by the more humble name Everett. Everett's odyssey begins on a work farm (he was sent up for practicing law without a license), where he is chained to two fellow convicts, Pete and Delmar. Needing to return home to prevent the marriage of his wife to another, Everett convinces Pete and Delmar to join him in his escape by telling them of a million-dollar treasure he buried after "knockin' off" an armored truck. The problem is that the site of the treasure is about to become the bottom of a lake: a river is being dammed in order to flood the valley, so there is some urgency to their adventure.

Like Homer's Ulysses, Everett and his crew encounter the usual suspects on their journey, including various versions of prophets, the Sirens, and a Cyclops. But what I find most intriguing in the film is an interesting—dare I say?—postmodern tension experienced by Ulysses Everett McGill. Everett is in many respects a devotee of modernity committed to a scientistic worldview. His trust is in reason, and like his Enlightenment forebears, he sees the traditions and "superstitions" of religion as an obstacle to true knowledge. When Pete and Delmar enter the waters of baptism and "get saved," Everett is incredulous and mockingly offers a quasi-Marxist account of the whole affair: "Well, I guess in hard times, flush the chumps! Everybody's lookin' for answers."[2] After Delmar's "been saved," he exhorts Everett: "You should've joined us, Everett. It couldn'ta hurt none." But Everett will have none of it: "Join you two ignorant fools in a ridiculous superstition?! [Mocking and smug:] Baptism! You two're just dumber than a bag o' hammers."

While Everett always concedes that "everyone's lookin' for answers," he is confident that those answers are found in reason and "abstract thought," not in divination.[3] The tales and fables of religion are to be overcome by the facts and propositions of science. However, Everett's modernist rationalism is challenged

2. The Cyclopean Bible salesman, Big Dan, shares this notion, taking advantage of the Depression to sell the Bible as an opiate for the impoverished masses. As he puts it, there's a big market for Bibles "in this time of woe and want. People are lookin' for answers."
3. Or women! As Everett commands Delmar: "Never trust a female. . . . Truth means nothing to a woman, Delmar. Triumph of the subjective!"

from beginning to end by a persistent religious and prophetic voice; his commitment to reason and science as the source of the answers everybody is looking for is called into question by the interruption of the divine, particularly by the tales and proclamations of a blind prophet. At the beginning of their journey they first encounter the blind prophet, who utters this revelation:

> I work for no man. I have no name. You seek a great fortune. You will find a fortune, though it will not be the fortune you seek. But first you must travel a long and difficult road—a road fraught with peril. You shall *see* things, wonderful to tell. You shall see a cow on the roof of a cotton house. I cannot tell you how long this road shall be. . . . Though the road may wind, yea your heart grow weary, still shall ye follow the way—even until your salvation.

Everett, as you would expect, responds with skepticism. "What the hell does he know? He's an ignorant old man." Throughout the story, Everett continues to resist the interruptions of the divine, seeing them as superstitions and silly stories in contrast to the facts and discoveries of science and rationality. But in the final chapters of the narrative, Everett's rationalism seems to meet its match.

After being pardoned by the governor of Mississippi and recapturing the love of his beloved Penelope, Everett has just one task remaining: to retrieve the wedding ring from their cabin. But when he arrives at the cabin, waiting for him and his companions is the diabolical warden, who has been pursuing them since their escape—the "devil" of the film who is interested not in proclamations of pardon but only in finishing his task: the execution of Everett, Delmar, and Pete. "End of the road, boys," he hisses. "It's had its twists and turns. . . . You have eluded Satan, you have eluded me for the last time. . . . Perhaps you should start making your prayers," he mocks, tossing three nooses over the tree branch.

Pete launches into fervent prayers, beseeching God for mercy and forgiveness. And then, slowly, Everett descends to his knees and begins to pray. Everett, the devotee of modernity and master of suspicion, prays: "Please look down on us poor sinners. I just want to see my daughters again, Lord. I'm sorry. . . . Help us, Lord. Let me see my daughters again, Lord." At the conclusion of the prayer, water begins trickling through the dust surrounding their feet, and a rumbling can be heard in the distance, growing louder and louder. Suddenly, an Exodus-like wall of water comes crashing over the cabin, first sweeping away the devil/warden and then carrying out Everett, Delmar, and Pete. As they emerge to the surface, Delmar exclaims: "A miracle! That was a miracle!"

"Delmar, don't be ignorant," Everett replies. "I told you they was floodin' this valley."

"No, that ain't it," Delmar responds.

"We prayed to God, and he pitied us," Pete adds.

"Well, it never fails," Everett remarks. "Once again you two hayseeds are showin' how much you want for intellect. There's a perfectly scientific explanation for what just happened."

"That ain't the tune you were singing back there at the gallows!" Pete reminds him, to which Everett responds with a modernist soliloquy: "Well, any human being will cast about in a moment of distress. No, the fact is they're floodin' this valley so they can hydro-electric up the whole darn state. Yessir, the South is going to change—everything is going to be put on electricity and put on a payin' basis. Out with the spiritual mumbo jumbo, the superstitions, and the backward ways. We're gonna see a brave new world where they run everybody a wire and hook us up to a grid. Yessir, a veritable age of reason, like the one they had in France. Not a moment too soon." Just then, Everett sees a disconcerting sight: a cow on the roof of a cotton house.

Everett Ulysses McGill is never quite disabused of his (religious) commitment to modernity. Despite the persistent challenges to his scientist faith, he clings to the religion of the Enlightenment. The film leaves the viewer with the responsibility for decision, as it closes with the blind prophet making his way down the tracks.

Lyotard's Claim: Postmodernism Is Incredulity toward Metanarratives

Postmodernism can be understood as the erosion of confidence in the rational as sole guarantor and deliverer of truth, coupled with a deep suspicion of science—particularly modern science's pretentious claims to an ultimate theory of everything.

As such, Ulysses Everett McGill embodies modernity, but a modernity now haunted, from beginning to end, by the otherwise-than-rational—the blind prophet making his way on the railroad. In a way, then, we see a tension between a modern, scientistic worldview, on the one hand, and an ancient-postmodern, mythic worldview, on the other. This is true to our own experience: we have not emerged into a radically new postmodern world; rather, our modern world is disrupted and haunted by postmodern suspicions and critique. Our time is a bit like downtown Los Angeles, whose architecture reflects both epochs. It is not that the postmodern has come in and flattened the modern; rather, the curvaceous lines and eclectic ensembles of Frank Gehry's postmodern architecture assert themselves alongside the modernist glass boxes and crumbling "projects" inspired by Le Corbusier.

It is just such a tension and conflict between science and narrative that situates Jean-François Lyotard's account of postmodernism. Lyotard was one of the first to have the courage to attempt a definition of the new creature postmodernism. Writing a "report on knowledge" commissioned by the government of Quebec, Lyotard opened his analysis with the claim: "Simplifying to the extreme, I define *postmodern* as incredulity toward metanarratives."[4] The French term (curiously) translated by "metanarratives" is *grand reçits*, big stories. Postmodernism, then, is the suspicion of and disbelief in "big stories." Now, if ever there was a big story, it is the grand narrative offered in Scripture, spinning a tale from before creation until the consummation of time (and beyond). Thus, if postmodernism is incredulity toward metanarratives, and Christian faith as informed by the Scriptures is just such a metanarrative, then postmodernism and Christian faith must be antithetical: postmoderns could never believe the Christian metanarrative, and Christians should not participate in postmodernism's incredulity. As with Derrida, Lyotard's claim and orthodox Christian faith are often

---

4. Jean-François Lyotard, *The Postmodern Condition: A Report on Knowledge*, trans. G. Bennington and B. Massumi (French original, 1979; Minneapolis: University of Minnesota Press, 1984), xxiv; henceforth abbreviated in the text as *PC*. For a more detailed, scholarly account of Lyotard's argument, see my "Little Story about Metanarratives: Lyotard, Religion, and Postmodernism Revisited," *Faith and Philosophy* 18 (2001): 353–68.

understood to be mutually exclusive. And we find such a reading suggested by even the most nuanced Christian commentators on postmodernity.[5]

However, this judgment is a bit hasty—another myth that needs to be demythologized. It is a bumper-sticker reading of Lyotard that is not informed by a careful understanding of just what Lyotard means by a metanarrative. As such, it also misunderstands what it would mean no longer to believe in metanarratives—to be incredulous with respect to metanarratives. This chapter more carefully engages Lyotard's critique and demonstrates that Christians should find in Lyotard not an enemy but an ally: orthodox Christian faith actually requires that we, too, stop believing in metanarratives.

The first thing we need to do, then, is define the term "metanarrative"—or more specifically, get a clear handle on Lyotard's definition of the term. Only then can we understand his claim that postmodernism is incredulity toward metanarratives. Generally, it is thought that the term refers simply to big stories—grand, epic narratives (*grand réçits*) that tell an overarching tale about the world. In other words, many assume that metanarratives are the target of postmodern disbelief because of their scope, because they make grand, totalizing claims about reality and have universal pretensions.[6] In other words, as Merold Westphal suggests, metanarratives would simply be meganarratives.[7] If that were the case—that any grand story with a global scope were a metanarrative—then, indeed, the biblical narrative of creation, fall, redemption, and eschatological consummation would be a legitimate object of postmodern suspicion and incredulity.

But this is not what Lyotard means by a metanarrative. What is at stake for Lyotard is not the scope of these narratives but the nature of the claims they make. Put another way, the problem isn't the stories they tell but the way they tell them (and, to a

---

5. I am thinking of Richard Middleton and Brian Walsh's otherwise excellent book, *Truth Is Stranger Than It Used to Be* (Downers Grove, IL: InterVarsity, 1995). A similar understanding of the antithesis between postmodernism and Christianity is offered by Stanley Grenz, Henry H. Knight III, and Brian Ingraffia.

6. See, for instance, Middleton and Walsh, *Truth Is Stranger*, 70–71.

7. Merold Westphal, *Overcoming Onto-Theology: Toward a Postmodern Christian Faith* (Bronx, NY: Fordham University Press, 2001), xiii.

degree, why they tell them). For Lyotard, metanarratives are a distinctly modern phenomenon: they are stories that not only tell a grand story (since even premodern and tribal stories do this) but also claim to be able to legitimate or prove the story's claim by an appeal to universal reason. Thus for Lyotard, the purveyor of metanarratives in *O Brother, Where Art Thou?* would be not the religious believers or prophets but rather the enlightened man of science, Ulysses Everett McGill. It is the supposed rationality of modern scientistic stories about the world that makes them a metanarrative. On Lyotard's account, Homer's *Odyssey*—though telling a grand story and making universal claims about human nature—is not a metanarrative because it does not claim to legitimate itself by an appeal to a supposed universal, scientific reason; rather, it is a matter of proclamation, or kerygma, which demands the response of faith. On the other hand, the scientific stories told by modern rationalism (Kant), scientific naturalism, or sociobiology are metanarratives insofar as they claim to be demonstrable by reason alone.

The central tension for Lyotard is not between big stories and little stories or global narratives versus local narratives. Instead, he formulates the tension as a conflict between science and narratives: when judged by the criteria of modern science, stories and narratives are little more than fables. When pushed, however, science must legitimate itself: it must produce a discourse of legitimation, which Lyotard simply calls philosophy. Thus, before determining what *postmodern* means, he first defines what he means by *modern*: "I will use the term *modern* to designate any science that legitimates itself with reference to a metadiscourse of this kind making an explicit appeal to some grand narrative, such as the dialectics of Spirit [Hegel], the hermeneutics of meaning [Schleiermacher?], the emancipation of the rational [Kant] or working subject [Marx], or the creation of wealth [Adam Smith]" (*PC*, xxiii). The question of the relation between modernity and postmodernity revolves around this issue of "legitimation." Modernity, then, appeals to science to legitimate its claim—and by "science" we simply mean the notion of a universal, autonomous reason. Science, then, is opposed to narrative, which attempts not to prove its claims but rather to proclaim them within a story.

The Myth of Truth and the Truth of Myth

But postmodernism, according to Lyotard, has suggested that the emperor of modernity has no clothes! At the heart of the postmodern critique of modernity is an unveiling of the way that science—which is so critical of the "fables" of narrative—is itself grounded in a narrative. What modernity did not recognize about itself was the way in which narrative infiltrated science. Lyotard makes a distinction between "narrative knowledge" and "scientific knowledge"—the latter being distinctively modern, the former being both premodern and postmodern. He makes the same distinction by talking about the difference between science and myth (or "traditional knowledge"). Narrative knowledge is grounded in the custom of a culture and, as such, does not require legitimation. Lyotard links this to a tribal paradigm in which the homogeneity of a people (*Volk*), coupled with the authority of a narrator, produces a kind of immediate auto-legitimation.[8] "The narratives themselves have this authority," he notes. In a sense, "the people are only that which actualizes the narratives" (*PC*, 23). Legitimation in terms of demonstration is not demanded but rather is implicit in the narrative itself as a story of the people.

In contrast to this auto-legitimation, modern scientific culture externalizes the problem of legitimation. Lyotard explains this in terms of the pragmatics of communication, where a speaker who makes a truth claim is a "sender," and the receiver or hearer of this claim is an "addressee." The two pragmatic poles of sender and addressee are distinguished, and the addressee demands of the sender justification for messages sent her way. I, as sender, must now provide "proof" (*PC*, 23–24). However, because the homogeneity of the premodern *Volk* has dissolved, we have no immediate or previously agreed-on consensus. In Lyotard's terms,

8. It is hard to resist comparing this to John Calvin's account of the *autopistie*, or self-authentication, of Scripture (see *Institutes*, I.vii.5). This is why Michael S. Horton, in *Covenant and Eschatology: The Divine Drama* (Louisville: Westminster John Knox, 2002), has suggested that Calvin and the post-Reformation scholastics were, in a sense, "postfoundationalist" theologians. For a historical account, see Richard A. Muller, "Sources of Reformed Orthodoxy: The Symmetrical Unity of Exegesis and Synthesis," in *A Confessing Theology for Postmodern Times*, ed. Michael Horton (Wheaton: Crossway, 2000), 43–62.

we do not all share the same language game. As such, modern legitimation has recourse to a universal criterion: reason—a (supposedly) universal stamp of legitimation. This move generates what Lyotard famously describes as metanarratives: appeals to criteria of legitimation that are understood as standing outside any particular language game and thus guarantee universal truth. And it is precisely here that we locate postmodernity's incredulity toward metanarratives: they are just another language game, albeit masquerading as the game above all games. Or as Lyotard puts it, scientific knowledge, which considered itself to be a triumph over narrative knowledge, covertly grounds itself in a narrative (i.e., an originary myth).

In particular, Lyotard analyzes two modern narratives of legitimation: first, the humanistic metanarrative of emancipation (as found in Kant and Marx), and second, the metanarrative concerning the life of the Spirit in German Idealism. One could perform similar analyses of rationalist market economics or the steady rise of sociobiology from Darwin onward. But we can already see this infusing of myth[9] in knowledge as far back as Plato, where "the new language game of science posed the problem of its own legitimation at the very beginning" (*PC*, 28). In books 6 and 7 of the *Republic*, for instance, the answer to the question of legitimation (here both epistemological and sociopolitical) "comes in the form of a narrative—the allegory of the cave, which recounts how and why men yearn for narratives and fail to recognize knowledge. Knowledge is thus founded on the narrative of its own martyrdom" (*PC*, 28–29). In a similar way, Lyotard argues, modern scientific knowledge, when called on (by itself) to legitimate itself, cannot help but appeal to narrative—this "return of the narrative in the non-narrative" is "inevitable" (*PC*, 27–28). Like the loquacious Ulysses Everett

9. "Myth" here should not be understood in the modern, scientistic sense as a "fable" opposed to truth; instead, it indicates the religious, confessional status of a truth. We should understand myth here in the sense also suggested by C. S. Lewis. According to Lewis, the imagination is a truth-bearing faculty that communicates not via propositions but via myths. Myths allow us to experience "as a concrete what can otherwise be understood only as an abstraction." See C. S. Lewis, "Myth Became Fact," in *God in the Dock: Essays on Theology and Ethics*, ed. Walter Hooper (Grand Rapids: Eerdmans, 1970), 67. My thanks to Kevin Vanhoozer for pointing me to this Lewis source.

McGill, modernity and its science can't stop telling stories (is there a bigger story than *On the Origin of Species?*)—all the while claiming that they are opposed to such "fables." Scientists and modern philosophers still tell stories; as Lyotard comments, "the state spends large amounts of money to enable science to pass itself off as epic" (*PC*, 28). Whenever science attempts to legitimate itself, it is no longer scientific but narrative, appealing to an orienting myth that is not susceptible to scientific legitimation. Modernity's science demands of itself the impossible: "The language game of science desires its statements to be true but does not have the resources to legitimate their truth on its own" (*PC*, 28). The appeal to reason as the criterion for what constitutes knowledge is but one more language game among many, shaped by founding beliefs or commitments that determine what constitutes knowledge within the game; reason is grounded in myth. "Metanarratives," then, is the term Lyotard ascribes to these false appeals to universal, rational, scientific criteria—as though they were divorced from any particular myth or narrative. For the postmodernist, every scientist is a believer.

Here we must return to the question posed earlier: If postmodernity is incredulity toward metanarratives, then does postmodernism signal a rejection of Christian faith insofar as it is based on the grand story of the Scriptures? The answer is clearly negative, since the biblical narrative and Christian faith claim to be legitimated not by an appeal to a universal, autonomous reason but rather by an appeal to faith (or, to translate, myth or narrative). That said, some might argue that the Christian faith can be legitimated by reason. In evangelical apologetic discussions, for instance, classical or evidential apologists (versus presuppositionalists) might argue that Christian faith is grounded in reason and thus constitutes a metanarrative. Without rehearsing the history of debates regarding apologetic method, I would argue that classical or evidentialist apologetics would fall prey to Lyotard's critique of metanarratives (since it consorts with a notion of universal reason), and that such a critique would be welcomed by presuppositionalists. One of the constructive engagements with Lyotard would be to consider his discussion of language games and critique of metanarratives and its correlation with presuppositional discourses on worldviews and the critique of autonomous reason.[10] To put it another way: classical apologetics is quite distinctly modern in its understanding of knowledge and truth.

Lyotard very specifically defines metanarratives as universal discourses of legitimation that mask their own particularity; that is, metanarratives deny their narrative ground even as they proceed on it as a basis. In particular, we must note that the postmodern critique is not aimed at metanarratives because they are really grounded in narratives; on the contrary, the problem with metanarratives is that they do not own up to their own mythic ground. Postmodernism is not incredulity toward narrative or myth; on the contrary, it unveils that all knowledge is grounded in such. Once we appreciate this, the (false) dichotomy that Middleton and Walsh, Grenz, Ingraffia, and others propose is dissolved insofar as the biblical narrative is not properly a metanarrative. As a result, new space is opened for a Christian appropriation of the postmodern critique of Enlightenment rationality.

What characterizes the postmodern condition, then, is not a rejection of grand stories in terms of scope or in the sense of epic claims, but rather an unveiling of the fact that all knowledge is rooted in *some* narrative or myth—an insight earlier made by Schaeffer and Van Til. The result, however (and here I note one of the genuine problems of postmodernity), is what Lyotard describes as a "problem of legitimation" (*PC*, 8) (or what Habermas describes as a "legitimation crisis") since what we thought were universal criteria have been unveiled as just one game among many. If we consider, for instance, the reality of deep moral diversity and competing visions of the good, postmodern society is at a loss to adjudicate the competing claims. There can be no appeal to a higher court that would transcend a historical context or a language game, no neutral observer or "God's-eye view" that can legitimate or justify one paradigm or moral language game above another. If all moral claims are conditioned by paradigms of historical commitment, then they cannot transcend those conditions; thus every moral claim operates within a "logic" that is conditioned by the paradigm. In other words, every language game

10. For a nuanced discussion of the latter, see Herman Dooyeweerd, *In the Twilight of Western Thought: Studies in the Pretended Autonomy of Theoretical Thought*, ed. James K. A. Smith, Collected Works, B/4 (Lewiston, NY: Edwin Mellen Press, 1999).

has its own set of rules. As a result, criteria that determine what constitutes evidence or proof must be game relative: they will function as rules only for those who share the same paradigm or participate in the same language game. The incommensurability of language games means that there is a plurality of logics that precludes any demonstrative appeal to a common reason. Recognition of the incommensurability of language games and the plurality of competing myths means that there is no consensus, no *sensus communis*. Many—especially Christians—lament this state of affairs (hence the renaissance of natural-law theories that purport to find a common ground for all). But is this situation as bad as we think? Are we lamenting the loss of what was a very modern hegemony of America, for instance? Is our situation really all that different from the situation of the apostle Paul or Augustine? Should we be trying to establish a common myth for an entire nation—a Constantinian strategy—or should the church simply be a witness amid this plurality of competing myths? (We'll return to these questions below.)

In the face of this problem, we must not lose sight of the fact that what constitutes the postmodern condition is precisely a plurality of language games—a condition in which no one story can claim either universal auto-legitimation (because of the plurality of "the people") nor appeal to a phantom universal reason (because reason is just one myth among others, which is itself rooted in a narrative). And this plurality is based on the fact that each game is grounded in different narratives or myths (i.e., founding beliefs). Whether we understand this as a new Babel or a new Pentecost, this situation—though posing a challenge—also presents a unique opportunity for Christian witness in postmodernity. The Ulysses Everett McGills will persist in our day, but postmodernism also opens the space for the faith narratives of a Delmar.

Taking Lyotard to Church

Having corrected the bumper-sticker understanding of postmodernism as incredulity toward metanarratives and seeing the way in which postmodernism, according to Lyotard, calls into question rationalist understandings of knowledge, we've begun to recognize the way in which postmodernism opens the space for Christian witness to be bold in its proclamation, its narration of the story. While in modernity science was the emperor who set the rules for what counted as truth and castigated faith as fable, postmodernity has shown us the emperor's nudity. As such, we no longer need to apologize for faith—we can be unapologetic in our kerygmatic proclamation of the gospel narrative. Thus the postmodern critique of metanarratives echoes Schaeffer and Dooyeweerd's earlier criticisms of the autonomy of reason. As such, Lyotard's analysis and critique of metanarratives have two important implications for Christian faith and the life of the church.

The Faith-full-ness of Our Knowledge

At root, what is at stake in postmodernism is the relationship between faith and reason. When Lyotard describes postmodernism as incredulity toward metanarratives, he indicates a suspicion and critique of the very idea of an autonomous reason, a universal rationality without ultimate commitments. Modernity's metanarratives cannot disengage themselves from narratives as their ultimate ground and thus cannot divorce themselves from myth, orienting beliefs that themselves are not subject to rational legitimation. In this light, consider, for instance, Thomas Kuhn's analysis concerning the role of paradigms in scientific research. Dominated by the language of faith,[11] Kuhn's *Structure of Scientific Revolutions* points out the role of paradigms as "constellations of belief"[12] that orient how we perceive our world and determine what we consider knowledge and truth. In other words, science finds itself grounded in prior beliefs that do not admit of legitimation but rather function as the basis for further legitimation. The paradigm itself is a belief, a matter of faith. It is also at this level that Wittgenstein notes: "If I have exhausted the justifications I have reached bedrock, and my spade is turned. Then I am inclined to say: 'This is simply what I do.'"[13] To this list we could add Ga-

11. For just a selective example of such passages, see Thomas Kuhn, *The Structure of Scientific Revolutions*, 2nd ed. (Chicago: University of Chicago Press, 1970), on belief, see 2, 4, 17, 43, 113; on commitments, see 4–5, 7, 11, 40–43; on tradition, see 6, 10, 39, 43.

12. Ibid., 175.

13. Ludwig Wittgenstein, *Philosophical Investigations*, trans. G. E. M. Anscombe (New York: Macmillan, 1959), §217.

damer, Polanyi, Derrida, and others; common to all of them is a delimitation of rationality, particularly Enlightenment ideals of scientific, objective rationality.

In this sense, the postmodern critique described by Lyotard as incredulity toward metanarratives represents a displacement of the notion of autonomous reason as itself a myth. And that is a project with which Christians ought to ally themselves, particularly once we have clarified that such an alliance does not require jettisoning the biblical narrative. By calling into question the idea of an autonomous, objective, neutral rationality, I have argued that postmodernity represents the retrieval of a fundamentally Augustinian epistemology that is attentive to the structural necessity of faith preceding reason, believing in order to understand—trusting in order to interpret.[14] While this Augustinian structure is formalized—in the sense that there is a plurality of faiths, as many as there are language games—the structure (of faith preceding reason) remains in place, in contrast to modern (and perhaps even Thomistic)[15] epistemologies (theories of knowledge).

The incredulity of postmodernity toward metanarratives derives from the fact that modernity denies its own commitments, renounces its faith, while at the same time never escaping it. Postmodernism refuses to believe the Enlightenment is without a creed. But note: the postmodern critique demands not that modern thought relinquish its faith (a modern gesture, to be sure) but that it own up to it—openly confess its credo. Thus we might consider the postmodern critique as a revaluing of myth, of orienting faith, providing new spaces for religious discourse—and in particular,

14. See my "The Art of Christian Atheism: Faith and Philosophy in Early Heidegger," *Faith and Philosophy* 14 (1997): 71–81; and idem, "Is Deconstruction an Augustinian Science? Augustine, Derrida, and Caputo on the Commitments of Philosophy," in *Religion with/out Religion: The Prayers and Tears of John D. Caputo,* ed. James H. Olthuis (London: Routledge, 2002), 50–61.

15. As Francis Schaeffer suggested in *Escape from Reason,* the notion of an autonomous reason is not unique to the Enlightenment but can already be located in Aquinas's understanding of natural reason. Aquinas and Augustine disagree on this point, as seen in Aquinas's commentary on Boethius's *De trinitate,* Q. 1, art. 1. My goal here is not to mediate that debate but to raise a question that demands further consideration. For an argument to the contrary, see John Milbank and Catherine Pickstock, *Truth in Aquinas,* Radical Orthodoxy Series (New York: Routledge, 2001).

an integrally Christian philosophy—in a climate where it has been demonstrated that everyone's "got religion."

How will this insight be helpful to Christian scholars and thinkers? My point is not to suggest that Lyotard's analysis concretely helps us understand Christian faith; in other words, I am not arguing that we look to Lyotard for assistance in understanding Christian faith commitments. Rather, Christian thinkers should find in Lyotard's critique of metanarratives and autonomous reason an ally that opens up the space for a radically Christian witness in the postmodern world—both in thought and in practice. By calling into question the very ideal of a universal, autonomous reason (which was, in the Enlightenment, the basis for rejecting religious thought) and further demonstrating that all knowledge is grounded in narrative or myth, Lyotard relativizes (secular) philosophy's claim to autonomy and so grants the legitimacy of a philosophy that grounds itself in Christian faith. Previously such a distinctly Christian philosophy would have been exiled from the "pure" arena of philosophy because of its "infection" with bias and prejudice. Lyotard's critique, however, demonstrates that no philosophy—indeed, no knowledge—is untainted by prejudice or faith commitments. In this way the playing field is leveled, and new opportunities to voice a Christian philosophy are created. Thus Lyotard's postmodern critique of metanarratives, rather than being a formidable foe of Christian faith and thought, can in fact be enlisted as an ally in the construction of a Christian philosophy.

But beyond the implications for Christian scholarship, this postmodern critique of metanarratives has important effects for Christian ministry and public witness. To the extent that the postmodern critique is effective, the modern notions of a neutral public space and secular sphere must be abandoned.[16] The exclusion of faith from the public square is a modern agenda; postmodernity should signal new openings and opportunities for Christian witness in the broad marketplace of ideas. We must be careful, however, not to continue to propagate that witness in modernist ways: by attempting our own rationalist demonstrations of the truth of Christian faith and then imposing such on a pluralist culture (what is

16. For an insightful analysis of these secular "bully" strategies, see Stephen L. Carter, *The Culture of Disbelief: How American Law and Politics Trivialize Religious Devotion* (New York: BasicBooks, 1993).

often described as a Constantinian agenda). The new apologetic of postmodernity will echo the patient presuppositionalist apologetic of Schaeffer—getting everyone's presuppositions on the table and then narrating the story of Christian faith, allowing others to see the way in which it makes sense of our experience and our world. While the new apologetics will be an *un*apologetics, it will at the same time be characterized by faithful storytelling, not demonstration. It must be kerygmatic and charismatic: proclaiming the story of the gospel in the power of the Spirit.

The Narrative Character of Our Faith

Too many Christians are just pious versions of Ulysses Everett McGill; that is, too many Christians have bought into the modernist valorization of scientific facts and end up reducing Christianity to just another collection of propositions. Our beliefs are encapsulated in "statements of faith" that simply catalog a collection of statements about God, Jesus, the Spirit, sin, redemption, and so on. Knowledge is reduced to biblical information that can be encapsulated and encoded.[17] And so, in more ways than one, our construal of the Christian faith has capitulated to modernity and what Lyotard calls its "computerization" of knowledge, indicating a condition wherein any knowledge that cannot be translated into a simple "code" or reduced to "data" is abandoned (*PC*, 4).[18] But isn't it curious that God's revelation to humanity is given not as a collection of propositions or facts but rather within a narrative—a grand, sweeping story from Genesis to Revelation? Is there not

17. This can been seen in quite a remarkable way in D. A. Carson, *Becoming Conversant with the Emerging Church: Understanding a Movement and Its Implications* (Grand Rapids: Zondervan, 2005), chap. 7: "Some Biblical Passages for Evaluation." The chapter is a collection of lists of proof texts that are supposed to have the self-evident force of criticizing "hard postmodernism" just by documenting the texts—a sort of miniconcordance of Bible verses that use the words "true" or "truth." Carson's critique of McLaren on this score, particularly on questions of narrative (ibid., 163–66), is an epic adventure in missing the point.

18. This "propositionalization" of the gospel is also anti-missional. If all the "facts" or "data" of the gospel are "out there," so to speak, then there is nothing more to be done. However, if narration and enactment are central, then mission is central and ongoing. My thanks to Bill VanGroningen for a conversation on this point.

a sense in which we've forgotten that God's primary vehicle for revelation is a story unfolded within the biblical canon?

By pointing to the fundamentally narrative basis of all knowledge, Lyotard reminds us about the ultimately narrative character of Christian faith. This resonates with postliberal theology (as found in the work of Stanley Hauerwas, for example), which emphasizes the narrative character of revelation.[19] Why is narrative important, and how does it differ from propositional knowledge? First, narrative is a more fully orbed means of communication (and hence revelation), activating the imagination and involving the whole person in a concrete world where God's story unfolds. Second, Christian faith—unlike almost any other world religion (with the exception of Judaism)—is not a religion simply of ideas that have been collected. The faith is inextricably linked to the events and story of God's redemptive action in the world: Christian faith rests on the work of the Word, who "suffered under Pontius Pilate," and that work can only be properly proclaimed by being narrated, by telling a story. The notion of reducing Christian faith to four spiritual laws signals a deep capitulation to scientific knowledge, whereas postmodernism signals the recovery of narrative knowledge and should entail a more robust, unapologetic proclamation of the story of God in Christ. This is why the Scriptures must remain central for the postmodern church, for it is precisely the story of the canon of Scripture that narrates our faith.

The narrative character of our faith should affect not only our proclamation and witness but also our worship and formation. Although I focus on the question of formation in chapter 3, here I want to emphasize the way in which Christian worship should reenact the narrative of the gospel week by week in order to teach us how to find ourselves in the story. Crucial for our discipleship and formation is being able to write ourselves into the story of God's redeeming action in the world—being able to find our role in the play, our character in the story. To do that, we need to know the story, and that story should be communicated when we gather as the people of God, that is, in worship. This is why the most postmodern congregations will be those that learn to be ancient,

19. See also the recent call to recover this theme in Michael S. Horton, *Covenant and Eschatology: The Divine Drama* (Louisville: Westminster John Knox, 2002) and Kevin J. Vanhoozer, *The Drama of Doctrine: A Canonical-Linguistic Approach to Christian Theology* (Louisville: Westminster John Knox, 2005).

reenacting the biblical narrative.[20] Just as Lyotard's account of narrative knowledge shows a link between premodern and postmodern, so worship in postmodernity (which appreciates the role of narrative) should signal a recovery of liturgical tales—the narrating of creation, fall, redemption (as well as crucifixion, burial, and resurrection) in the very manner in which we worship.[21]

A Storytelling Church

How should the church look different after this encounter with Lyotard and postmodernism? What implications does this have for practice? Building on our initial tour of a deconstructive church in chapter 2, as well as suggestions in this chapter, let's continue our tour of the postmodern church by visiting a "storytelling" church. What's happening?

Again, we find that the role of Scripture is central, not just as the Text that mediates our understanding of the world but also as the Story that narrates our role in it. Each week the worshipping community is confronted by the narrative of a God who makes a covenant with his people, who is faithful to his promises, and who acts in history to effect a relationship with his people.[22] The story of Yahweh unfolds as the drama of salvation—a drama in which Yahweh is the "star"[23] but also in which each of us finds a role. In order to appreciate the breadth of this story, each week the postmodern church narrates "scenes" from the different "acts" of the drama: a scene from the Old Testament, a scene from the Gospel narratives, and a scene from the Epistles.[24]

20. Robert Webber has suggested something similar in *Ancient-Future Faith: Rethinking Evangelicalism for a Postmodern World* (Grand Rapids: Baker, 1999).

21. I would note the work of Marva Dawn as crucial for reflection on the theology of worship.

22. For a rich account of the story of the God who acts, see Michael Horton, *Covenant and Eschatology*.

23. That is, worship is about the glory of God, not the satisfaction of one's needs. For a discussion that recovers the centrality of God as the focus of worship, see Michael S. Horton, *A Better Way: Recovering the Drama of God-Centered Worship* (Grand Rapids: Baker, 2002).

24. Building on the use of the lectionary in chapter 2, which would help the community cover the entirety of the story over time, not just our favorite scenes.

But in addition to the narration of the story in Word, this post-modern church narrates the story in its practices. Like the early church (Acts 2:42; 20:7), this postmodern community celebrates communion each week, for in the celebration of the Eucharist it narrates the gospel: the death, burial, and resurrection of the Lord Jesus Christ, which enacted a new covenant between God and his people. In this act of eating and drinking, the community proclaims the Lord's death "until he comes" (1 Cor. 11:26). While the postmodern church is a storied community centered on the narrative of Scripture, it is also a eucharistic community that replays the narrative in deed. Further, the symbols and signs of the Lord's Supper embody the gospel for us. Because the postmodern church values narrative, it values story and as such values the aesthetic experience engendered by material signs and symbols. Put another way, because of the renewed role of story as a kind of literature activating the imagination, the postmodern church values the arts in general as an incarnational medium that embodies the story of God's faithfulness. Seeing iconoclasm as a symptom of a kind of modern Platonism, the postmodern church affirms the role of the aesthetic (what plays on the senses) in telling the story. Just as God communicates to humanity through the incarnation of the Word as flesh—the image of the invisible God (Col. 1:15)—so God continues to speak to the church through the material symbols of bread and wine but also through images and dance.[25]

The postmodern church resists the tendency of pragmatic evangelicalism, which tries to "dumb down" the story to make it accessible or attractive to the culture. Instead, the postmodern church affirms the timelessness (and timeliness) of the biblical narrative as it is told. Rather than trying to translate the biblical story into a contemporary, more "acceptable" narrative (which usually ends up compromising the narrative to culture), the postmodern church seeks to initiate listeners into the narrative. Authentic Christian worship both invites outsiders into the gospel story and provides a significant means for the formation of disciples of Jesus Christ. In other words, authentic worship does not have to choose between reaching seekers and building

25. We will return to a fuller consideration of aesthetics and liturgy in chapter 5.

up the saints. Incarnational worship does both. As the Church of Scotland's *Common Order* of worship puts it, public worship is both a "converting ordinance" and "an edifying ordinance";[26] that is, worship can be both a way of inviting the lost into the body of Christ and a way of building up the saints, forming them into the kinds of people that pursue the kingdom with heart, soul, mind, and strength.

Worship, then, needs to be characterized by hospitality; it needs to be inviting. But at the same time, it should be inviting seekers into the church and its unique story and language.[27] Worship should be an occasion of cross-cultural hospitality. Consider an analogy: When I travel to France, I hope to be made to feel welcome. However, I don't expect my French hosts to become Americans in order to make me feel at home. I don't expect them to start speaking English, ordering pizza, talking about the New York Yankees, and so on. Indeed, if I wanted that, I would have just stayed home! Instead, what I'm hoping for is to be welcomed into their unique French culture; that's why I've come to France in the first place. And I know that this will take some work on my part. I'm expecting things to be different; indeed, I'm looking for just this difference. So also, I think, with hospitable worship: seekers are looking for something our culture can't provide. Many don't want a religious version of what they can already get at the mall. And this is especially true of postmodern or Gen X seekers: they are looking for elements of transcendence and challenge that MTV could never give them. Rather than an MTVized version of the gospel, they are searching for the mysterious practices of the ancient gospel.

Quinn Fox recently captured this point with a brilliant analogy between Starbucks and the church. The church, he suggests, "might learn about corporate worship language from the language of coffee. Starbucks realizes, it seems, that a distinctive menu that people need to learn is not a bad thing." In his

---

26. On this point, see William Storrar, "From *Braveheart* to Faint-Heart: Worship and Culture in Postmodern Scotland," in *To Glorify God: Essays on Modern Reformed Liturgy*, ed. Bryan Spinks and Iain Torrance (Grand Rapids: Eerdmans, 1999), 70–71.

27. On these matters, I am deeply indebted to Marva Dawn, *Reaching Out without Dumbing Down: A Theology of Worship for This Urgent Time* (Grand Rapids: Eerdmans, 1995).

testimony, he confesses: "I did not inherit my parent's commitment to coffee. Rather, 'I found it' in my late 30s." His coming to faith in coffee required learning a new language, the Italian parlance of Starbucks. But this wasn't off-putting to him; he didn't complain that it wasn't user friendly. Rather, he felt he was being invited into a world:

> At busy times an orderly (if slow) procession of the faithful crowd toward the counter. An order may be something like "I'd like a *grande*, non-fat, triple shot, 2 pump peppermint *latte* with extra whip cream." The money changer loudly relays the request. And one should not worry if the strangeness of the terms causes a stumble. The temple assistant mediates these early morning "sighs that are too deep for words" by translating them into flawless coffee Italian. The Barista (it even sounds a little like "priest") who feverishly prepares coffee drinks behind the espresso bar repeats the petition verbatim, as if by uttering the words s/he speaks them into being. At the more relational franchises, the customer's name will be attached to the order. When the brew is ready, complete in all of its uniqueness, the Barista chants the request once again, just to indicate that the unction is complete.[28]

Postmodern worship does something of the same: orienting itself by ancient, strange practices but in a way that invites not only the faithful but also the searching into the story's rhythms and cadences.

Finally, the postmodern church recognizes that its primary responsibility is to live the story for the world. The church is the stage where God's drama is played out; as such, we Christians have a responsibility to "act well," we might say, to faithfully play out the love of God in the church as a community of love and justice. Our storytelling should be supported by our story living.

---

28. See Quinn Fox, "Liturgy and Starbucks," *Perspectives* (February 2003). Online: http://www.perspectivesjournal.org/perspectives/2003/02/seeit-starbucks .php.

4

Power/Knowledge/Discipline

Foucault and the Possibilities
of a Postmodern Church

Michel Foucault's attention is drawn to institutions of power: prisons and schools, hospitals and factories, sex and money. What could he have to say to a postmodern church? In this chapter, we'll explore Foucault's claim that "power is knowledge" in order to see its insight into Christian formation and discipleship.

Raising the Curtain: *One Flew over the Cuckoo's Nest*

The hospital is a machine—that is Chief's thesis in *One Flew over the Cuckoo's Nest*.[1] The hospital is part of the Combine that "works over" individuals by means of its power, its control. The hospital's walls hum with the sound of its machinery of surveillance and repression—"hum of black machinery, humming hate

1. I will refer to the 1975 film directed by Milos Forman but also to the original novel by Ken Kesey (1962; repr., New York: Penguin, 1976). The novel is narrated in the first person from Chief's perspective.

and death and other hospital secrets."[2] On the mental ward of this Oregon hospital, Chief—a longtime resident—is able, in a way, to see through walls and can thus observe the hospital's machinations of power firsthand. Even the strategies aimed toward cure are in fact systems of control and domination: from the orderlies to the medication, from the strict schedule and work regimen to the "therapeutic circle" that serves only to humiliate—all performed to the tune of banal background music that functions as the soundtrack for repression.

At the center of the machine—but also an effect of it—is the watchful eye of Nurse Ratched. From the glass-enclosed nurse's station, she keeps watch over the ward like the warden from a prison watchtower. Indeed, the mental ward is a panopticon of sorts, a structure where a central hub of power is able to see all of those subjected to it, monitoring their actions sheerly by surveillance—by the threat of being seen. Nurse Ratched oversees this environment and employs all the tools of her trade to carry out her surveillance and punishment. Robotlike herself, Nurse Ratched is the eyes and ears of the machine, the agent of its disciplines. Every once in a while, Chief glimpses her real self, her inner workings, when "she really lets herself go and her painted smile twists, stretches to an open snarl, and she blows up bigger than a tractor, so big I can smell the machinery inside the way you smell a motor pulling too big a load."[3] But as Chief realizes, while Nurse Ratched is the face of the system, she is but a part of it: "It's not just the Big Nurse by herself," he concludes, "but the whole Combine, the nation-wide Combine that's the really big force, and the nurse is just a high-ranking official for them."[4]

Of course, Nurse Ratched does not speak or think of her work as surveillance and certainly not as punishment. The stated goal of the institution is healing and cure. Or, to stick with Chief's mechanistic metaphor, the hospital is a shop for repair—not quite manufacturing, since the specimens are brought into the shop, but rather remanufacturing, setting broken objects into a mold that knocks off the edges and makes them conform to the

2. Kesey, *One Flew over the Cuckoo's Nest*, 1. One could also compare the role of ducts in the film *Brazil*.
3. Ibid., 5.
4. Ibid., 181.

shape of societal expectations. The physicians are merely techni-
cians whose procedures are "installations" that are engineered
for cure. Sometimes the patient's wiring is so malfunctioning
that the hospital needs to reset the circuitry with a dose of high
voltage (electroshock therapy). Although some patients have an
initial concern, patient Daniel Harding explains that the goal of
the procedure is simply a microcosm of the goal of the institution: "In this country, when something is out of order, then the
quickest way to get it fixed is the best way." Responding to the
suggestion that this is similar to "electrocuting a guy for murder," Harding continues: "Both activities are much more closely
related than you think; they are both cures."[5]

What really concerns Chief, however, is not the regimen of
medicines and timetables, restraints and electroshock therapy.
What is of greater concern are the Combine's more covert opera-
tions, its stealth control and manipulation—the way it "works on
you" without your knowing it, the way it worked on Chief's father.
"They work on you ways you can't fight!" Chief warns. "They
install things. They start as quick as they see you're gonna be big
and go to working and installing their filthy machinery when
you're little, and keep on and on and on till you're *fixed!*"[6]

Wandering into the panopticon one day—into the clutches
of the Combine and Nurse Ratched—is Randle P. McMurphy,
shipped to the mental ward from a work farm at Pendleton.
What stands most in need of repair in McMurphy is the fact
that he doesn't think he needs repair. (McMurphy is committed,
whereas most of the other patients are in the ward voluntarily,
submitting to the repair work of therapy by choice.) McMurphy
becomes something of a project for Nurse Ratched, who sees that
he is a "manipulator" planning to "take over." But the Combine
and its emissaries will have none of that. The narrative of *One
Flew over the Cuckoo's Nest* recounts the struggle of the system
in its attempts to repair R. P. McMurphy and his resistance to
its power, which inspires others, like Chief, to resist its clutches.
But ultimately the story ends with the triumph of the system,
culminating in McMurphy's lobotomy, which leaves him a near
lifeless shell on the Acutes ward. (To prevent McMurphy's my-

5. Ibid., 179.
6. Ibid., 209.

thology from being tarnished, Chief smothers the now-docile McMurphy and, because of McMurphy's heroic resistance, finally musters the strength and drive to break through the glass of the mental ward and escape into the surrounding hills.)

The film and novel paint a vivid and disturbing picture of institutional power and its attempts to whitewash its mechanisms with paternalistic claims about "cure" and the "good of the patient." Although McMurphy is the hero because of his libido-driven resistance to the system, even his empowerment of the other patients cannot stop the driving cogs of the Combine: McMurphy, though mythologized, is crushed by the machine. Thus *One Flew over the Cuckoo's Nest* leaves us just where we would expect from a work dating from the 1960s: with a deep suspicion of institutions, institutional power, and the control they exert over us. We are left simply with the return of Nurse Ratched, the continued machinations of the hospital, and the remaining hum of the Combine in its walls. If we are to escape control and the trappings of institutional power, the only way out is to follow Chief through the shattered window, wandering alone, institutionless but "free."

Foucault's Claim: Power Is Knowledge

There is a sense in which Michel Foucault is the Randle P. McMurphy of our unholy trinity—a somewhat libido-driven[7] rebel, protesting control and resisting systems by documenting their covert domination in modern culture. If Forman's *One Flew over the Cuckoo's Nest* became something of a visual anthem for a generation, Michel Foucault's *Discipline and Punish* has become an analogous anthem for postmodernity across the disciplines, from criminal justice to education.[8] What is fascinating is the way in which Foucault's history of prisons says so

---

7. This is the (somewhat controversial) interpretation of Foucault offered by James Miller in his *Passion of Michel Foucault* (New York: Simon & Schuster, 1993). Miller argues that Foucault's theories reflect an outgrowth of his own experiential and experimental sexual escapades.

8. Michel Foucault, *Discipline and Punish: The Birth of the Prison*, trans. Alan Sheridan (French original, 1975; repr., New York: Vintage, 1977); henceforth abbreviated in the text as *DP*.

much about other institutions such as schools, factories, and hospitals. While we might expect the hospital of *One Flew over the Cuckoo's Nest* to mirror Foucault's specific analysis of hospitals in his earlier work *The Birth of the Clinic*,[9] the mental ward under Nurse Ratched's surveillance more resembles the carceral systems described in *Discipline and Punish*. Indeed, we need to appreciate that Foucault's account of the "birth of the prison" is not really about penitentiaries; it is about the way in which society as a whole reflects the prison. The prison is but a microcosm of society itself.

For Foucault, at the root of our most cherished and central institutions—hospitals, schools, businesses, and, yes, prisons—is a network of power relations. The same is true of our most celebrated ideals; at root, Foucault claims, knowledge and justice reduce to power. While we moderns—especially we moderns who grew up on "Schoolhouse Rock"—were shaped by the maxim of Francis Bacon proclaiming that "knowledge is power," Foucault's postmodern axiom is that "power is knowledge." However, Foucault himself resists any bumper-stickerization of this notion. As he clarifies, he does not mean that knowledge and power are identical;[10] instead, he means to emphasize the inextricable relationship between knowledge and power. Knowledge, or what counts as knowledge, is not neutrally determined.[11] Instead, what counts as knowledge is constituted within networks of power— social, political, and economic. As he states near the beginning of *Discipline and Punish*, we should give up the notion that power

9. Foucault, *The Birth of the Clinic: An Archaeology of Medical Perception*, trans. A. M. Sheridan Smith (French original, 1963; New York: Vintage, 1973). A second French edition appeared in 1972 and was published in English in 1994.

10. As Foucault puts it: "It has been said but you have to understand that when I read—and I know it has been attributed to me—the thesis, 'Knowledge is power,' or 'Power is knowledge,' I begin to laugh, since studying their *relation* is precisely my problem. If they were identical, I would not have to study them, and I would be spared a lot of fatigue as a result. The very fact that I pose the question of their relation proves clearly that I do not *identify* them" ("Critical Theory/Intellectual History," an interview reprinted in *Critique and Power*, ed. Michael Kelly [Cambridge, MA: MIT Press, 1994], 133).

11. This is why I suggest below that Foucault's "genealogy" shares something in common with presuppositionalist approaches to epistemology, which emphasize the role of "control beliefs" [Wolterstorff] in the constitution of knowledge.

leads to madness; quite to the contrary, "we should admit rather that power produces knowledge (and not simply by encouraging it because it serves power or by applying it because it is useful); that power and knowledge directly imply one another; that there is no power relation without the correlative constitution of a field of knowledge, nor any knowledge that does not presuppose and constitute at the same time power relations" (*DP*, 28). Thus Foucault regularly speaks of "power-knowledge relations" or the "nexus" of power/knowledge.

Like Chief in *One Flew over the Cuckoo's Nest*, postmodernism is characterized by a deep hermeneutic of suspicion.[12] This is why Foucault, following Nietzsche, describes his method in intellectual history as "genealogy" or "archaeology" whose task is to uncover the secret, submerged biases and prejudices that go into shaping what is called the truth.[13] There is no claim to truth that is innocent; there is no knowledge that simply falls into our minds from the sky, pristine and untainted. What might be claimed as obvious or self-evident is, in fact, covertly motivated by other interests—the interest of power. If someone says, "What do you mean? This is just the way things are. Can't you see that?" Foucault the genealogist traces the lineage of such thinking to the beliefs that really motivate it. Or to use his archaeological metaphor, he digs beneath the surface of what goes around as objective truth to show the machinations of power at work below the surface. Like Chief, who can see through the pristine white walls of the hospital to its more monstrous workings, Foucault sees through the neat and tidy claims to objective truth, seeing them as only masks of power. The genealogist, then, shares Chief's critical X-ray vision, and "finds that there is 'something altogether different' behind things: not a timeless essential secret, but the secret that they have no essence or that their essence was fabricated in a piecemeal fashion from alien

12. Christians, aware of the deep structural effects of sin, should also operate with a hermeneutics of suspicion, even if suspicion doesn't get the last (or first) word. For discussions along these lines, with an eye on practice, see Merold Westphal, *Suspicion and Faith* (Bronx, NY: Fordham University Press, 1998).

13. Foucault unpacks this method most carefully in his essay "Nietzsche, Genealogy, History," in *Language, Counter-Memory, Practice*, ed. Donald F. Bouchard (Ithaca, NY: Cornell University Press, 1977).

forms."[14] Like a genealogist whose patient documentation of a family tree shows the family's complicity in the evils of slavery, so Foucault's genealogy intends to show that modernity's claims to scientific objectivity or moral truth are fruits of a poisoned tree of power relations. Or to use an architectural metaphor, Foucault's archaeology sets out to show that what we thought were sure foundations are more like collections of fragments piled in the bottom of the hole.[15] Foucault is not out to lament this situation, as though we had lost our foundations, but rather to get us to own up to what has always been the case.

To claim that power is knowledge, then, is to make a claim about the power relations that stand behind both institutions and ideals. As Nietzsche earlier claimed in his *Genealogy of Morals*, good and evil are just names that we give to the power interests of the strong versus those of the weak. Thus "in a sense," Foucault concludes, "only a single drama is ever staged in this 'non-place,' *the endlessly repeated play of dominations.*"[16] The story of humanity is not the Enlightenment fiction of perpetual progress or the constant progression of the race, as Kant (and Richard Rorty) suggest, but rather simply the shift from one combat to another, from one form of domination to another.

Foucault's claim, however, is not a proclamation made from on high, as if it were just the kind of heaven-sent axiom he protests against. His claim about the relation between power and knowledge is not an a priori or abstract claim; rather, it is a claim that bubbles up from his analyses of concrete institutions and ideals such as hospitals and prisons, notions of madness versus reason, or the history of sexuality. Thus Foucault's claim is always made on the basis of case studies—where the axiom is not applied to a case but rather arises from it. If Foucault thinks that power is knowledge, it is because the history of modern institutions bears that out. Let us consider one of his case studies in more detail both to see how Foucault operates and to understand the context of his more general claim. I have chosen to focus on

14. Ibid., 142.
15. "The search for descent is not the erecting of foundations: on the contrary, it disturbs what was previously considered immobile; it fragments what was thought unified; it shows the heterogeneity of what was imagined consistent with itself" (ibid., 147).
16. Ibid., 150, emphasis added.

his most influential study—that of prisons offered in *Discipline and Punish*.

The Subject of Discipline

Foucault's account of the modern prison begins with a ghastly scene from 1757, recounting the punishment and execution of a regicide named Damiens. Wearing nothing but a shirt, he was conveyed in an oxcart "to the Place de Grève, where, on a scaffold that will be erected there, the flesh will be torn from his breasts, arms, thighs and calves with red-hot pincers, his right hand, holding the knife with which he committed the said parricide, burnt with sulfur . . . then his body drawn and quartered by four horses and his limbs and body consumed by fire, reduced to ashes and his ashes thrown to the winds" (*DP*, 3). As it turned out, six horses were eventually needed for this final operation, and "when that did not suffice, they were forced, in order to cut off the wretch's thighs, to sever the sinews and hack at the joints" (*DP*, 3).

Though we are horrified by the description of such an event orchestrated in the name of justice—and surely Foucault opens with just such an intention—we will properly understand Foucault's analysis only if we appreciate that, for him, modern society is in some sense worse than the one that tortured and executed Damiens. In other words, the thesis of Foucault's *Discipline and Punish* is that the society that tortured Damiens is less dangerous than the society that locked up Chief in that Oregon mental institution—that what Damiens suffered was, in some sense, less evil than what Randle P. McMurphy suffered. By the end of *Discipline and Punish*, Foucault wants us to be equally horrified by the mechanisms of domination that suffuse modern society.

This is why *Discipline and Punish*—like almost all of Foucault's case studies—is not ultimately about prisons but rather concerns modern society as a whole. If he documents a change in the strategies of punishment and discipline within the penal system, this is only a microcosm of broader movements in modern Western culture. Although the book is divided into three parts that trace the historical development of penal theory from torture (roughly, sixteenth and seventeenth centuries) to punishment (eighteenth century) and finally discipline (nineteenth and twentieth centuries), the underlying force of Foucault's descriptive argument is to show that there is no qualitative difference between these epochs—that, if anything, the later developments are somehow more brutal. The story of change in punishment is not a narrative of progress, let alone a story of the triumph of the humane, but rather the substitution of one form of domination for another (more insidious) mode of domination. Foucault is interested in narrating not just the subplot of the history of prisons but rather the story of how we got to where we are: a modern "disciplinary" society where all of us, like Chief and McMurphy, are subject to mechanisms of control and repression.

What interests me about Foucault is his analysis of the way in which society is put together by sinews of power—and that it could not be otherwise. A different configuration of society is just a different (and not necessarily better) constellation of forces of power. All three parts of the book are trying to lay out the "mechanisms of power" at work in the different epochs of penal history. In the epoch of torture, this power "works on" the criminal in order to produce a confession, because a confession produces the truth—inscribes the truth in and on the body of the condemned (*DP*, 37, 38, 39–40, 41). This was brought about by both public and ritual means (*DP*, 43). The confession meant the condemned agreed with his sentence, which justified his punishment. But what was the end of such a "production of truth"? To solidify the power of the sovereign (*DP*, 47–49, 50). This is why he concludes that truth is always a function of power and vice versa: "The truth-power relation remains at the heart of all mechanisms of punishment," and that is precisely what *"is still to be found in contemporary penal practice"* (*DP*, 55). At the core of Foucault's historical analysis is really a genealogy of the present.

A change did take place in how punishment is administered: eighty years after the torture and execution of Damiens, the model of punishment was no longer the rack but the regimen of discipline with its specification of rules and schedules (see *DP*, 6–7). According to Foucault, the changes were not motivated by a desire to be more humane (as is commonly supposed) but rather were a means of dealing with political (even revolutionary) problems that attended the public display of torture. What began to happen was the opposite of what was intended: instead of enforcing new allegiance to the king, the spectacles of torture tended to make the people identify with the criminal! So punishment gradually became less violent and more secret. A "new age for penal justice" dawned (*DP*, 7). But the result of this shift was a social cost: "Crimes seemed to lose their violence, while punishments, reciprocally, lost some of their intensity, *but at the cost of greater intervention*" (*DP*, 75, emphasis added). Crime was constructed differently, based on new economic structures (focusing on property rather than violence). This created a certain "class justice" (*DP*, 75). But what interests Foucault is the way in which this shift in crime also entailed new emphasis on control and prevention and "stricter methods of surveillance" (*DP*, 77).

Was penal reform really a change in attitude, the result of a new "humanism"? Foucault is suspicious (see *DP*, 78): "More certainly and more immediately, it was an effort to adjust mechanisms of power that frame the everyday lives of individuals; an adaptation and a refinement of the machinery that assumes responsibility for and places under surveillance their everyday behavior, their identity, their activity, their apparently unimportant gestures" (*DP*, 77). Such surveillance becomes synonymous with society itself, entailing "a closer penal mapping of the social body." The result—and this is decisive—was to "make punishment and the repression of illegalities a regular function, *coextensive with society*" (*DP*, 82). Foucault goes on to speak of this as the generalization of punishment—the extension of controlling mechanisms to society itself—and the rest of *Discipline and Punish* traces this spreading and suffusion of discipline in modern society.

Through the course of his analysis, Foucault documents the formation of what he calls a "disciplinary society"—the primary goal of which is the creation of the individual—a "reality fabricated by this specific technology of power that [he has] called 'discipline'" (*DP*, 194). So the goal of a disciplinary society, and the institutions within that society, is the formation of individuals by mechanisms of power. Society makes individuals in its own image, and the tools for such manufacturing are the disciplines of power. Here Foucault adds an important proviso: "We must cease once and for all to describe the effects of power in negative terms: it 'excludes,' it 'represses,' it 'censors,' it 'abstracts,' it 'masks,' it 'conceals.' In fact, power produces; it produces reality" (*DP*, 194). In Foucault's descriptive analyses, he does not attempt to offer any kind of evaluation of power as either positive or negative. But this does at least prohibit describing its effects as negative. For Foucault—and this is close to the heart of the theory of society offered in *Discipline and Punish*—power is necessary and constitutive of society. All that changes are the mechanisms and technologies of power. One could not have a society that is not fundamentally characterized by power relations.

As a case study of the disciplined society, Foucault asks us to compare the difference between the way medieval cities responded to disease and the way the early modern city responded to the plague. The "political dream" of a disciplinary society is found, in fact, in the historical organization of the plague-stricken town. Why? Because the plague-stricken town is the paradigmatic example of a regulated, disciplined organization of individuals subjected to constant surveillance and registration ("the gaze"): "a compact model of the disciplinary mechanism" (*DP*, 197). While the medieval case of the leper produced procedures of exclusion and isolation, "the [modern] plague gave rise to disciplinary projects" (*DP*, 198). "The first is that of a pure community, the second that of a disciplined society. Two ways of exercising power over men, of controlling their relations, of separating out their dangerous mixtures. The plague-stricken town . . . is the utopia of the perfectly governed city" (*DP*, 198). Note that here Foucault's conception of the nature of power comes to the surface: the two different modes (exclusion, discipline), insofar as they are manifestations of power, always involve power over others; power is always some form of control. But couldn't one conceive of power differently? We'll return to this question.

The organization of society around discipline (as a new mode of power) culminates in an "architecture" concerned with much more than buildings; it is an architecture for society itself that generalizes "the gaze." The architectural ideal is the panopticon envisioned by Bentham's model for a penitentiary. "The Panopticon must not be understood as a dream building: it is the diagram of a mechanism of power reduced to its ideal form; its functioning, abstracted from any obstacle, resistance, or friction, must be represented as a pure architectural and optical system: it is in fact a figure of political technology that may and must be detached from any specific use" (*DP*, 205). That is why, whether in Bentham's prison or in Nurse Ratched's mental ward, "whenever one is dealing with a multiplicity of individuals [i.e., society] on whom a task or a particular form of behavior must be imposed, the panoptic schema may be used" (*DP*, 205). Thus the panopticon gives rise to panopticism, the generalized mode of asymmetrical surveillance, of being seen without seeing:[17] "The panoptic schema . . . was destined to spread throughout the social body; its vocation was to become a generalized function" (*DP*, 207). The panopticon, then, far from being just an architectural ideal for the prison, was the utopian dream of a disciplinary society, "a generalizable mode of functioning; a way of defining power relations in terms of the everyday life of men" (*DP*, 205). Panopticism accomplishes the generalization of discipline throughout the social body.

Hence, "our society is one not of spectacle, but of surveillance" (*DP*, 217); that is, the generalization of discipline as constitutive of society itself ("coextensive with the entire social body," *DP*, 213) weaves observation and documentation into the warp and woof of society in order to create "docile" and "useful" subjects—of the state, of capitalism, and so on (*DP*, 216–17, 220–21). The disciplinary society forms individuals into what it wants them to be: docile, productive consumers who are obedient to the state. Like McMurphy in the hands of Nurse Ratched, we are "projects" in need of reengineering and repair. We are all like the residents of the mental ward, in the place of being supervised and controlled, watched over and dominated by structures of surveillance and discipline that have become suffused through society.

In the final section of *Discipline and Punish*, a very important shift in the analysis and argument of the book takes place: in a sense, we come back to the prison here, since the predominant focus of part 3 is not the prison but society as a whole. In other

17. One of the most important aspects of the panopticon was this asymmetry, which allowed the "subjects" to be seen but not the observers. The subject "is seen, but he does not see" (*DP*, 200). This invisibility of the observers also means that they need not always be observing: "for what matters is that he knows himself to be observed," that he might be the subject of observation at any moment (*DP*, 201). Cf. the words written on the cell walls at Mettray: "God sees you." The panopticon is the substitution for an omniscient deity (or Santa!).

words, part 3 traces the development of a disciplinary society. In part 4, Foucault suggests that the modern penitentiary is a product *of* a disciplinary society, rather than a disciplinary society being the reflection of penal practice. Thus, when we look at the modern penitentiary, we are looking at ourselves, seeing our society reflected in a mirror, as it were. The modern prison only codifies and localizes the generalization of discipline that has already been effected throughout the social body. It is not that the prison came to be a model for society; rather, the disciplinary mechanisms of society "colonized the legal institution" (*DP*, 231). If Foucault is documenting the birth of the prison, it is delivered from the matrix of a disciplinary society already in place. As an "apparatus for transforming individuals," the penitentiary "merely reproduces, with a little more emphasis, all the mechanisms that are to be found in the social body" (*DP*, 233)—in the military, schools, hospitals, and factories.[18] As he comments, "This prison came from elsewhere" (*DP*, 256). And later he concludes that the prison "continues, on those who are entrusted to it, a work begun elsewhere, which the whole of society pursues on each individual through innumerable mechanisms of discipline" (*DP*, 302–3). It is not that society has come to mimic prisons but rather that prisons are microcosmic crystallizations of what is characteristic of society itself. In modern society discipline is ubiquitous.[19]

This condition is analyzed through three particular regimens: isolation, compulsory labor, and treatment. Isolation is meant to bring the offender into confrontation with himself; it is a moral discipline. Work creates a laboring subject (proletarian) fit for a capitalist society, reformed to meet the requirements of the machines of production (*DP*, 242); it is an economic discipline. Treatment or reform is a means of transforming the abnormal into a normal individual, to "cure" his abnormality; it is a kind of medical discipline.[20] As such, the modern penitentiary is about much more than mere detention or deprivation of liberty. These are necessary "supplements" to detention (*DP*, 248). They inscribe the structures and disciplines of society onto the offender.

18. Foucault analyzes these other social institutions, especially in the chapter titled "Docile Bodies" (III.1).
19. This is powerfully illustrated in another film, *Brazil*.
20. One can see all of these at work in *One Flew over the Cuckoo's Nest*.

And it is this that gives birth to the delinquent as the target of reform—no longer a criminal or a monster, the offender is an "abnormality" (*DP*, 251–52). If the penitentiary is intended for the delinquent—the abnormal one—it is because the broader society has determined what counts as normal. In fact, this is almost precisely the theory of the "therapeutic community" on the ward in *One Flew over the Cuckoo's Nest*. As Chief recounts the theory, "A guy has to learn to get along in a group before he'll be able to function in a normal society; how the group can help the guy by showing him where he's out of place; how society is what decides who's sane and who isn't, so you got to measure up."[21]

The creation of the delinquent gets to the heart of what Foucault sees at work, not only in modern penal practices but also in modern society as a whole: disciplinary power aimed at normalization. In fact, at the conclusion of the chapter (and the book) we see what function *Discipline and Punish* is meant to serve: it is a book intended to "serve as a historical background to various studies of the power of normalization and the formation of knowledge in modern society" (*DP*, 308). Hence, the prison is just one of many (all?) modern institutions that tend "to exercise a power of normalization" (*DP*, 308). What is this power? And how do we arrive at this conclusion?

The historic penitentiary at Mettray represents the culmination of this "carceral" ideal, incorporating the omni-disciplinarity of "cloister, prison, school, regiment" (*DP*, 293; cf. III.1). It included all the elements of the panoptic ideal, to the extent that even the observers were subjected to discipline when they were "taught the art of power relations" (*DP*, 295). "In the normalization of the power of normalization, in the arrangement of a power-knowledge over individuals, Mettray and its school marked a new era" (*DP*, 296). This new era involved the widening of carceral circles to society itself: "The carceral archipelago transported this technique from the penal institution to the entire social body" (*DP*, 298). This in fact erased any kind of qualitative distinction between the "least irregularity" and the "greatest crime," since both, on this register, were to be considered "a de-

21. Kesey, *One Flew over the Cuckoo's Nest*, 47. All of this is undertaken under the banner of "democracy" (ibid.).

parture from the norm" (*DP*, 299). Rather than being an enemy of the sovereign or the social contract, "the social enemy was transformed into a deviant" (*DP*, 299)—hence the necessity for discipline and normalization from cradle to grave (*DP*, 300). The result is that nothing falls outside this carceral network: "There is no outside" (*DP*, 301). "In this panoptic society," Foucault observes, "of which incarceration is the omnipresent armature, the delinquent is not outside the law [there is no 'outlaw']; he is, from the very outset, in the law, at the very heart of the law, or at least in the midst of those mechanisms that transfer the individual imperceptibly from discipline to the law, from deviation to offence" (*DP*, 301). In fact, he seems to suggest that the deviant is a product of society.

This widening of the carceral circle means that society is characterized not by a disjunction between the social and the carceral but rather by a "carceral continuum" (*DP*, 303) that operates on the basis of a new law, the norm. Normalizing power thus spreads: "Borne along by the omnipresence of the mechanisms of discipline, basing itself on all the carceral apparatuses, it has become one of the major functions of our society. The judges of normality are present everywhere" (*DP*, 304). So the political issue at stake in the question of the prison is not about whether it is corrective or not: "The problem lies rather in the steep rise in the use of these mechanisms of normalization and the wide-ranging powers which, through the proliferation of new disciplines, they bring with them" (*DP*, 306). And it is precisely these powers of normalization that are the object of Foucault's concern.

Will the Real Foucault Please Stand Up?

So far I have summarized Foucault's case study in which he tries to concretely demonstrate the way in which power is knowledge or, more specifically, the necessary and ubiquitous role of power in society and social institutions. However, the next question is: Just what are we supposed to do with this analysis? Just why is Foucault painting this picture? What does he want us to conclude from this? What is Foucault trying to convince us of? After Foucault has powerfully described the development of modern, disciplinary society, what does he want us to do with

this? Is this intended simply as a neutral, objective description
of the way things are? As we've seen, such a notion runs counter
to Foucault's own notion of genealogy. Is there, then, behind
this description a latent prescription? Or, to put it otherwise, is
Foucault painting this intricate picture for us to show us what's
wrong with modern society? Is his work a protest—a call for
liberation from such repressive structures?

Here we hit on a difficult matter of interpretation, not just
for outsiders but even for Foucault scholars: Who is the real
Michel Foucault?[22] Is he some kind of modern—an ultimately
Enlightenment thinker committed to the autonomy and freedom
of the individual? Is he a Marxist protesting the abuse of power
and the oppressive structures of society? Is he a closet classic
liberal who is lashing out against anything that would restrict the
freedom and autonomy of the individual? These questions also
place another question on the table: If Foucault is a postmodern thinker, just how modern is postmodernism? (And later we
face another set of questions concerning just how far Christians
can go in appropriating the Enlightenment project of freedom.)
There are two basic ways that Foucault can be read in light of
these questions:

1. *The Nietzschean Foucault.* On this reading, Foucault's analyses are not intended to convey any kind of moralizing
   stance. In other words, the Nietzschean Foucault is not
   painting this picture of power to show that power is bad
   and should thus be undone. If Foucault is a Nietzschean, his
   project is purely descriptive and not intended to harbor any
   kind of prescription: he is just showing us the way things
   are, not how they're supposed to be. If one started to talk
   about power as bad or to think about one organization of
   society as better than another, then one would be invoking a
   system of values. But as Foucault's own exposition of Nietzsche demonstrates, for him all such values only reduce to
   power.[23] Beyond Foucault's own confessed Nietzscheanism,
   one can cite other evidence for this reading. It is certainly

22. It is not accidental that David Macey's landmark biography is titled *The
Lives of Michel Foucault*, in the plural.
23. See Foucault, "Nietzsche, Genealogy, History."

the case that Foucault does not think that power is bad; unlike Lord Byron, he does not think that power necessarily corrupts. As we've already seen, Foucault thinks we should stop talking about power in negative terms of repression and exclusion and instead think of it positively in terms of production. The Nietzschean Foucault would be trying not to change the world but only to describe it, perhaps even to celebrate it.

2. *The Liberal or Enlightenment Foucault.* Marx famously remarked that whereas philosophers usually just interpret the world, the point is to change it. The other way to read Foucault is to see him working in this broadly modern or Enlightenment tradition that includes both Kant and Marx. And, in fact, Foucault himself later acknowledged that he saw himself as a kind of Enlightenment thinker working in the tradition of critical theory stemming from Kant, through Marx, up to the Frankfurt School of Jürgen Habermas and others.[24] In that case, the way to read Foucault is to see him giving us this disturbing picture of control and domination in order to motivate us to change things. The evidence for this reading of Foucault (which I think is the better one) is twofold: On the one hand, we have external evidence, such as Foucault's own activist involvement in prison reform movements in France. On the other hand, the very language of *Discipline and Punish* already seems to communicate a negative evaluation of the way things are, eliciting a call for reform and revolution. When he describes particular configurations of power relations as networks of domination, such a descriptor already seems to entail an evaluation. A critical theory needs criteria. Indeed, the very notion of a neutral description of things runs counter to the core of Foucault's thought (and, as we've already seen, Derrida's too).

While there is certainly ambiguity on this score, the best reading of Foucault is to read him as a kind of closeted Enlightenment thinker; in fact, later in his work Foucault "comes out" on just

---

24. Foucault articulates this very clearly in lectures and interviews collected in *The Politics of Truth*, ed. Sylvère Lotringer (New York: Semiotext[e], 1997).

this point.[25] Moreover, this is certainly the way that Foucault has been *used*—as a protest thinker, co-opted by various versions of the political left in order to resist the continued vestiges of control and domination in modern culture. As such, Foucault has been adopted by various movements—from gay rights to educational reform—that protest any form of control over the individual.

If Foucault is a kind of covert Enlightenment liberal, what does that mean? First, we need to specify what we mean by "liberal" here: a classical political liberal who places priority on the individual as a sovereign, autonomous agent—a being who is lord of his or her domain and thus resists any mode of external control. The watchword of liberalism is freedom: the free agent should not be controlled—by a king, by tradition, by religion, or by institutions. So the liberal's slogan is varying versions of "Hands off! Don't try to control what I think; don't try to control what I believe; don't try to control what I do."[26] Any institution that tries to control beliefs or behavior is inherently dominating and repressive. And since institutions tend to be erected for just these reasons, there is a deep sense that institutions per se are structures of domination. Hence, liberalism in this sense is deeply anti-institutional; while leftists—whether politicos or filmmakers—speak about being radicals, it is usually a radical-izing of this Enlightenment notion of freedom. Thus there is a deeply libertarian streak to liberalism that eschews control and discipline. The very goal of Enlightenment is liberation, which is why both Kant and Marx are Enlightenment thinkers. And insofar as Foucault's work feeds into just such impulses, it is hard not to see a libertarian streak in his descriptions.

Just as it is difficult not to side with McMurphy in the face of the grinding repression of the Combine and Big Nurse, so it is difficult not to be sympathetic to Foucault's suspicion about

25. See especially the lectures collected in *The Politics of Truth*.

26. The term *liberal* is used in a more restrictive sense in American political parlance. But it is important to recognize that, with respect to the tradition of political liberalism I am describing here, both Democrats and Republicans are liberals. It is just that their "Hands off!" stances apply to different things: a Democrat is more likely to assert, "Hands off my body—I can do what I want with it!"; a Republican is more likely to assert, "Get your grubby tax-collecting hands off my money—it's mine to do what I want with it!" These are two points on the same liberal continuum.

institutions of discipline and formation. But I would argue that Christians should resist the temptation to side with either Mc-Murphy or Foucault (but neither should they side with Nurse Ratched or Mettray). On the other hand, Foucault provides some critical insights into the nature of discipline and its role in the formation of individuals. Thus my engagement with Foucault is complicated, as is my criticism. The critical point is that Foucault is absolutely right in his analysis of the way in which mechanisms of discipline serve to form individuals, but he is wrong to cast all such discipline and formation in a negative light. In other words, Christians should understand discipline positively, precisely because Christians should not be liberals in the classical sense described above. Christians should eschew the very notion of an autonomous agent who resists any form of control. By rejecting Foucault's liberal Enlightenment commitments, but appropriating his analyses of the role of discipline in formation, we can almost turn Foucault's project on its head.

Is Power All Bad?

If I have so far argued that Foucault is a kind of closet liberal and thus deeply modern, I need to be equally critical of evangelical (and especially American) Christianity's modernity and its appropriation of Enlightenment notions of the autonomous self. Indeed, many otherwise orthodox Christians, who recoil at the notion of theological liberalism, have unwittingly adopted notions of freedom and autonomy that are liberal to the core. Averse to hierarchies and control, contemporary evangelicalism thrives on autonomy: the autonomy of the nondenominational church, at a macrocosmic level, and the autonomy of the individual Christian, at a microcosmic level. And it does not seem to me that the emerging church has changed much on this score; indeed, some elements of emergent spirituality are intensifications of this affirmation of autonomy and a laissez-faire attitude with respect to institutions.[27] We don't

27. Although I am sympathetic to his critique, I worry, for instance, that Spencer Burke's critique of the church has absorbed some version of this penchant for liberal autonomy. See Spencer Burke, "From the Third Floor to the Garage," in *Stories of Emergence: Moving from Absolute to Authentic* (Grand Rapids:

want denominations to tell us how to run our churches, and we don't want churches to tell us how to run our lives. If either of these institutions threatens our autonomous sphere with control—let alone discipline—we jump ship: the church splits from the denomination to become an independent congregation, or the individual leaves the church and hops to another. So when we see the experience of Chief and McMurphy, because of our own (American) liberal suspicions about institutions and institutional control, we identify with these anti-institutional figures—all in the name of freedom (even if we also talk in terms of "law and order").[28]

But it is crucial to distinguish truly biblical conceptions of positive freedom and empowerment from liberal Enlightenment conceptions of negative freedom as a kind of hands-off stance. To put it a little more staunchly: freedom is an idol of the contemporary church, and we will only properly resist Foucault's liberalism if we give up our own.

Let me anticipate an initial response: Why should Christians resist these liberal conceptions of freedom? How can I be against freedom? Am I going to offer a defense of domination? If we're opposed to liberal conceptions of freedom, doesn't that mean we're *for* control and domination?

Well, yes. But in order for me to show why this isn't a revival of fascism, let's return to Foucault's conception of power. As Foucault describes it, social institutions and relationships are necessarily constructed on the basis of power relations; power is ubiquitous. Moreover, power is understood as power over others—some kind of domination (even if it isn't a simple bifurcation of haves and have-nots, those with power and those

Zondervan, 2003), 27–39. I worry that what is being offered is a spiritual version of Chief's escape from the institution into the "freedom" of the wilderness.

28. That said, we should also honor the complexity of situations that give rise to nondenominational churches. Some, no doubt, emerge from denominations that have become so static and modern that the denomination is no longer a link to the catholic tradition but rather a reified modernist institution. Not all denominations represent a link to the great catholic tradition; this is especially true of anti-creedal Protestant denominations that emerged in modernity. Vis-à-vis these, nondenominational congregations could actually provide the opportunity to be more catholic. However, nondenominational churches must grapple with how to connect with the *normativity* of the catholic tradition. My thanks to Brian McLaren for helping me to complexify these matters.

without).[29] This power is channeled through mechanisms of discipline—various practices and regimens—that form the individual by conforming him to what society wants—a good worker and consumer. And while he cautions that we should not think of this negatively, the overwhelming impression of his work is that this situation is both repressive and oppressive.

But should we accept this negative view of power? Is power all bad? Specifically, can Christians share in this devaluation of power and discipline as inherently evil? Can we who claim to be disciples—who are called and predestined to be conformed to the likeness of the Son (Rom. 8:29)—be opposed to discipline and formation as such? Can we who are called to be subject to the Lord of life really agree with the liberal Enlightenment notion of the autonomous self? Are we not above all called to subject ourselves to our *Domine* and conform to his image? Of course, we are called not to conform to the patterns of "this world" (Rom. 12:2) or to our previous evil desires (1 Peter 1:14), but that is a call not to nonconformity as such but rather to an alternative conformity through a counterformation in Christ, a transformation and renewal directed toward conformity to his image. By appropriating the liberal Enlightenment notion of negative freedom and participating in its nonconformist resistance to discipline (and hence a resistance to the classical spiritual disciplines),[30] Christians are in fact being conformed to the patterns of this world (contra Rom. 12:2).

Once we reject the liberal conception of the autonomous agent who resists control and discipline, Foucault's analyses of the mechanisms of discipline take on a very different light. Admittedly, Foucault seems to suggest that modern society simply took over religious disciplines and rituals and generalized or altered them. Thus he suggests that modern factories resemble medieval

29. This is why Foucault tends to resist being described as a Marxist; he thinks the Marxist conception of power in society is too simplistic, boiling down to a structure of haves and have-nots. But for Foucault, even the oppressors are effects of power, just as Nurse Ratched is an effect of the system, a product of the Combine.

30. The very notion of spiritual disciplines remains foreign and even anathema to many evangelicals. However, there are signs of a shift, engendered in large part by Richard J. Foster's classic, *Celebration of Discipline: The Path to Spiritual Growth* (San Francisco: Harper & Row, 1978).

monasteries (*DP*, 149), that modern prisons bear the marks of earlier convents (*DP*, 243), and that the general structures of a disciplinary society mimic monastic communities (*DP*, 149). And insofar as the prisons and factories of a disciplinary society are seen as repressive and dominating, the charge flows back against these earlier communities of religious discipline.

How can we respond to this charge? Of course, on the one hand, this simply flows from Foucault's liberalism, his opposition to domination and control as such. Insofar as we don't accept such a conception of the autonomous self, the criticism doesn't hold. But more importantly, on the other hand, this raises a crucial point: while formally or structurally speaking, there are mechanisms of discipline operative in both the convent and the prison, in both the factory and the monastery, more specifically these disciplines and practices are aimed at very different ends. And here we must make an important distinction: we can distinguish good discipline from bad discipline by its *telos*, its goal or end. So the difference between the disciplines that form us into disciples of Christ and the disciplines of contemporary culture that produce consumers is precisely the goal they are aiming at. Discipline and formation are good insofar as they are directed toward the end, or telos, that is proper to human beings: to glorify God and enjoy him forever (Westminster Catechism, question 1). Or, to put it otherwise, a disciplinary form is proper when it corresponds with the proper end of humanity, which is to be (renewed) image bearers of God. So other forms of disciplinary formation are bad and wrong insofar as they try to mold human beings into something other than what they are called to be. Almost universally these other modes of discipline are reductionistic because they reduce human beings to something less than they are called to be. Some modes of discipline reduce us to economic animals whose primary end is production and consumption; other modes of discipline reduce us to sexual animals whose primary end is instinctual satisfaction; still other modes of disciplinary society try to mold us into violent creatures whose primary end is destruction. What is wrong with all these disciplinary structures is not that they are bent on forming or molding human beings into something, but rather *what* they are aiming for in that process. Thus it is helpful to distinguish the formal *structure* of disciplinary formation as such from the specific *direction* discipline takes.[31] Admittedly, as we've learned in previous chapters, what constitutes the proper end, or telos, of human formation depends on the ultimate story we tell of what human beings are and what humans are called to be. The Christian story specifies that human beings are creatures whose ultimate telos is to image their Creator and be conformed to the image of his Son. Different stories obviously envision different ends for humanity. So what constitutes good or proper formation must be determined in relation to the particular founding narrative that we confess tells the truth about the world and the human condition. As such, we can draw an important link between Lyotard's emphasis on the role of narrative and Foucault's emphasis on the role of formation: discipline is aimed at formation for a specific end, and that end is determined by our founding narrative.

Taking Foucault to Church

Unlike our engagements with Lyotard and Derrida, there is a temptation for Christians to side with Foucault because much of modern Christianity has unwittingly bought into the Enlightenment notion of autonomy. As such, if we're going to put Foucault's analysis to work in shaping a postmodern church, we have to stand him on his head a bit: we need to see what he describes but reject what he thinks about disciplinary society as such. If we do that, what exactly does Foucault give us? In what way can he be a catalyst for thinking about a postmodern church?

The Cultural Power of Discipline Formation

Keep in mind that Foucault offers studies of all kinds of practices (from bells ringing to get us to move according to timetables to the use of negative stimuli to get us to stop doing something)

31. For a nuanced, brilliant account of these matters, drawing on Foucault, see Daniel M. Bell Jr., *Liberation Theology after the End of History: The Refusal to Cease Suffering*, Radical Orthodoxy Series (London: Routledge, 2001). I discuss this in some detail in *Introducing Radical Orthodoxy: Mapping a Post-secular Theology* (Grand Rapids: Baker, 2004), 243–54.

that shape and mold human beings to act in a certain way—to be certain kinds of persons. Foucault is absolutely right about the fact that this works! Disciplinary mechanisms in our society *do* make humans into certain kinds of people who are aimed at particular goals. For instance, many Americans are defined by the primary goal of consumption. They stake their identity on their material possessions—on labels, objects of luxury, and the never-ending process of keeping up with trends. If we look at the way upper-middle-class Americans spend their time and money, we have to conclude that their ultimate goal is to be faithful consumers. How did they get to be that way? How did they become that kind of person? The answer isn't simple, but we can easily identify several disciplinary practices that form human beings into these consuming animals.

First, the very success of capitalism depends on a consuming culture as market, and particularly a culture that wants ever-new products (otherwise the market becomes quickly saturated and the possibilities of profits quickly diminish). Thus we have a culture—or at least a class within the culture—that has a vested interest in seeing a society of consumers. How does it create this population of consumers? One of the primary ways has been the advent of mass media, which, from its inception, has been aimed at marketing. We must understand, for instance, that television programs were basically invented to gain an audience for commercials. Thus the majority of mass media is undertaken as a means for creating an audience for advertising that will eventually become a market of consumers. Marketing, then, is driven by investing products with social, sexual, and even religious value, which makes them something much more than they are.[32] In other words, marketing capitalizes on fundamental structural human desires for meaning and transcendence and presents products and services as ways to satisfy these human longings. It then utilizes the tools of disciplinary practice to inject these values into the very character of human beings—internalizing

---

32. For a very helpful and insightful discussion of the religious nature of advertising, see Charles Colson and Nancy Pearcey, *How Now Shall We Live?* (Wheaton: Tyndale House, 1999), chap. 23. See also Jean Kilbourne, *Can't Buy My Love* (New York: Free Press, 2000); and her video series *Still Killing Us Softly*; and James B. Twitchell, *Adcult U.S.A.: The Triumph of Advertising in American Culture* (New York: Columbia University Press, 1996).

the values so that they become part of the person. By using repetition, images, and other strategies—all of which communicate
truths in ways that are not cognitive or propositional—marketing
forms us into the kind of persons who want to buy beer to have
meaningful relationships, or buy a car to be respected, or buy the
latest thing to come along simply to satisfy the desire that has
been formed and implanted in us. It is important to appreciate
that these disciplinary mechanisms transmit values and truth
claims, but not via propositions or cognitive means; rather, the
values are transmitted more covertly, as Chief recognized. They
are communicated by a world of images and through a range
of practices that teach the body, as it were. This covertness of
the operation is also what makes it so powerful: the truths are
inscribed in us through the powerful instruments of imagination and ritual.

It is absolutely crucial that the church recognize this process.
In other words, the first thing we need to learn from Foucault is
how pervasive disciplinary formation is within our culture—from
public education to MTV. Anyone who raises children will with
some degree of reflection recognize that this is the case. Nothing
frustrates me more than the "label idolatry" already evident in my
children. Indeed, raising children in American culture has made
me see and appreciate the forces of disciplinary formation, and
the globalization of American values makes this a reality around
the world. All of us certainly find ourselves in multiple webs of
power relations and subject to multiple disciplinary mechanisms
bent on forming us into certain kinds of people. In the world
of late-modern capitalism, many of these disciplinary interests
coalesce. So those disciplinary mechanisms that would form us
into primarily sexual animals have been co-opted by capitalist
interests that want to form us into consumers. Everything from
beer and deodorant to shampoo and rice is sold on the basis of
sex. By unveiling the cultural power of disciplinary formation,
Foucault can be a catalyst for the scales falling from our eyes
so that we see what is happening.

The Necessity of Counterformation by Counterdisciplines

But beyond simply recognizing that such cultural formation
is pervasive, we also need to recognize that the telos, or goal, at

which these disciplines aim is fundamentally inconsistent with (and even competing with) the message of the gospel and what it specifies as the proper end of humanity. We need to recognize the inconsistency between how late-modern capitalism defines human beings and how Christian faith defines us. Because of the covertness of this formation, Christians are often not alert to what they are becoming. To use a metaphor that George Barna employed for quite different ends: Christians are sometimes like frogs in a kettle. Reportedly, if you place a frog in a pot of room-temperature water and gradually increase the temperature of the water, even to the boiling point, the frog will not jump out of the kettle, even if it means death. This is either because the frog doesn't sense the change, or because the change is so gradual it lulls the frog into accepting the environment. So also with the church: because the disciplinary mechanisms of Disney, MTV, and the Gap are so insidious and covert, we don't recognize the way in which their message—and their vision of the human telos—is shaping our own identity. Christians need first to recognize that disciplinary formation takes place in culture, then second, to recognize the antithesis between the dominant culture's understanding of the human calling and the biblical understanding of our ultimate vocation.

But the church must also do a third thing: enact counter-measures, counterdisciplines that will form us into the kinds of people that God calls us to be. Too often we imagine that the goal of Christian discipleship is to train us to think the right way, to believe the right things. But the ultimate goal of sanctification and discipleship is to shape us into a certain kind of person: one who is like Jesus, exhibiting the fruit of the Spirit (Gal. 5:22–23), loving God and neighbor, caring for the orphan, the widow, and the stranger (Jer. 22:3; James 1:27). He has shown us what is good and what the Lord requires of us: to do justice, to love mercy, and to walk humbly with God (Mic. 6:8). These are all just translations of the broader human vocation, which is to bear the image of Christ as renewed image bearers of God. The primary aim of discipleship is to create a certain kind of person who acts in a certain way, not someone who simply thinks in a certain way. According to the Scriptures, knowing the truth is only instrumental to ultimately doing the truth (Jer. 22:16).

But how do we become that kind of people? How do I become the kind of person who "does" the truth? It takes practice. First, it requires grace. Because no one is good (no, not one!), being properly directed to our proper telos requires a regeneration and redirection of the heart by the Holy Spirit. That is why they are fruits of the Spirit. Insofar as the Spirit indwells believers, they are being formed into the image of Christ to the extent that they learn to walk in the Spirit and in the Spirit's power. However, while regeneration is a necessary condition for becoming this kind of person, it is not a sufficient condition. This must be cultivated by practices of sanctification.

Second, recognizing the structural goodness of disciplinary formation, the church must utilize disciplines that will form us into these kinds of people—disciplines that will counteract the formation of MTV and television commercials. We would do well to recover the tradition of spiritual disciplines such as prayer and fasting, meditation, simplicity, and so on as a means of shaping our souls through the rituals of the body. Further, as I've already suggested, our corporate worship should be aimed at constituting us as disciples who are countercultural agents of redemption. Communion and confession, foot washing and economic redistribution are ways of practicing what it means to be citizens of the kingdom. And such practices inscribe this telos of the kingdom into our character.[33] Christian worship is one of the primary arenas in which we participate in the practices that shape who we are. If our worship simply mimics the disciplinary practices and goals of a consumer culture, we will not be formed otherwise. Conceiving of the church as a disciplinary society aimed at forming human beings to reflect the image of Christ, we will offer an alternative society to the hollow formations of late-modern culture.

33. For further discussion of worship as a means of forming character, see Marva Dawn, *Reaching Out without Dumbing Down: A Theology of Worship for This Urgent Time* (Grand Rapids: Eerdmans, 1995), chap. 6; Stanley Hauerwas, *The Peaceable Kingdom: A Primer in Christian Ethics* (Notre Dame: University of Notre Dame Press, 1983), 107–10; and Smith, *Introducing Radical Orthodoxy*, 235–39.

5

Applied Radical Orthodoxy
A Proposal for the Emerging Church

> We have seen that postmodern thought can be an occasion for a recovery of ancient Christian themes and sources because the critique of modernity reopens a significant role for tradition. In this chapter we will consider the unique connections between tradition and postmodernism by examining the voice of Radical Orthodoxy.

Raising the Curtain: *Whale Rider*

If there is one thing that postmodernism is opposed to, it is the traditional. The very notion of the postmodern has become synonymous with the new, the novel, the *avant-garde*, and at the very least, the contemporary. But is it possible to be faithful to tradition in the contemporary world? Is that even something we should want? Don't the advances of modernity—instantaneous global communication, the virtual connection of the four corners of the world, the steady march of technological mastery, the fluidity of trends and self-invention—don't these represent the overcoming of tradition and an escape from its static past? Who would want to go back to crawling when we've learned to fly? Or could it be that the price of flying is not worth the so-called freedom? Might the progressive, ahistorical detachment of our modern life be a denial of something that is part of the fabric of being human? Could it be that we are traditioned creatures, in which case unhooking ourselves from tradition would end only in self-alienation, even self-destruction?

These tensions between tradition and contemporary culture are powerfully illustrated in the film *Whale Rider*.[1] The film opens with the words "In the old days . . . ," then immediately cuts to the very modern, technological scene of childbirth in a contemporary hospital. The film's opening is both ancient and future: appealing to "the ancestors" while documenting the birth of the next generation. This ancient-future tension is what drives the narrative, centered around the young girl Paikea.

Whale Rider tells the story of a Maori tribe struggling to flourish in the Eastland region of New Zealand. The Maori have not weathered modernity well: the "opportunities" it has presented to the youth have produced something of a lost generation. Some, like Porourangi (the firstborn who should be chief-in-waiting), have welcomed the possibility of international travel as a way to escape the restrictions and expectations of a traditional culture. His younger brother, Rawiri, like other young men in the tribe (such as Hemi's father) has also escaped, but into a world of drug-induced immobilization and dilapidated squalor. In response to this rejection of Maori identity—particularly the rituals and "old ways" of the tribe—the chief, Koro, has responded with a retrenched commitment to recover the tradition in its most stringent form, further alienating his sons, Porourangi and Rawiri.

Koro has pinned all his hopes on Porourangi's firstborn, who, as the film opens, is being delivered into this world with much difficulty. This son, he believes, will be "the One" who will recover the power of the ancestors and redirect the Maori community—a prophet who will lead them. But the birth of this baby boy results in the death of his mother—only for the son to die moments later. Porourangi has lost his wife and son; Koro

1. *Whale Rider*, DVD, directed by Niki Caro (Culver City, CA: Columbia TriStar Home Entertainment, 2003).

has lost his hope. And lost in this tumult of grief and shattered hopes, a twin has arrived: a baby girl, ignored by her grandfather and later abandoned by her father. But in his confrontation with his father—who in the presence of Porourangi's dead wife could only ask, "Where's the boy?"—Porourangi has the audacity (and the hope?) to tell Koro his daughter's name: "Her name is Paikea," he announces.

"What?" Koro responds.

"You heard me."

"No, not that name."

Why Koro's horror on this announcement? Because the name both retrieves and challenges the heart of Maori tradition. The narrative or myth that orients the tribe revolves around the story of an ancient Paikea who, when his canoe capsized in the South Pacific, rode on the back of a whale to the Eastland region of New Zealand. Since that time, the tribe's chiefs have been the firstborn, male descendants of Paikea. For Porourangi to announce that his daughter would be called Paikea, when his firstborn son and rightful heir had died, was, from Koro's perspective, an act of defiance and a patent rejection of the traditions of the ancestors. And indeed this was Porourangi's last act before abandoning the island—and his responsibilities as firstborn—altogether, leaving the baby Paikea in the care of a loving grandmother but a disdaining grandfather, or Paka. In the face of Koro's rigid understanding of the tradition, Porourangi's only option is rejection and abandonment: he leaves his daughter, he escapes the tribe, and in a powerful symbol throughout the film, he leaves on the shore an unfinished *te waka*, or war canoe. Once the object of his artistic gifts and passion and a powerful expression of the tribe's tradition, the half-finished hulk of a vessel sits abandoned on the coastline—left to the elements but still having an intimidating presence that haunts the tribe. While they have sought to reject and forget their heritage, the massive, empty hull just won't go away.

When we next see the young Paikea, we find her in a tortured relationship with her Paka—tortured on both sides (for Paikea refuses to stop loving her grandfather). On the one hand, Paka can't seem to stop loving Paikea, playing with her on his bike, smiling gently into her face; on the other hand, his passion for the revival of the tribe through a new leader—firstborn and male—is frustrated every time he calls Paikea's name. She represents to him his own failure, and he worries that she is the sign that the tribe has been abandoned by the ancestors; indeed, he sees Paikea as bad luck. With the death of the firstborn male, the line of chiefs has returned to the ancestors, and Koro must find some way to get it back—some way to retrieve the charism of chief in someone. But he knows that can't be Paikea: the charism of chief could never be given to a girl.

So Koro undertakes measures to try to retrieve the tradition: he gathers all the firstborn males of the village and launches a sacred school meant to form them in the ancient ways. Paikea is systematically excluded, even told to stay off the grounds of the *marae*, or temple, because it is, according to Koro, "the one place where our old ways are upheld." In this sacred school of learning, they are taught the old ways: the chants and songs of the tribe, its stories and myths, its dances and rituals. The young boys find these old ways strange vis-à-vis the modernity in which they feel most comfortable. This is seen, for instance, in a ritual war dance where the boys are taught to slap their chests "until they bleed" and to stick out their tongues in the face of the opponent. "When you stick out your tongue," Koro explains, "you're saying to your enemy, 'I'm going to eat you.'" The boys, bewildered, are tentative to enter the practice.

They do take to one of the practices: a ritual form of combat using long staffs. Their formation in modernity has fostered a certain interest in violence, even if ritualized. Paikea, excluded from the training, tries to mimic the actions from a distance, using a broom handle. When Koro finds out, he hastily banishes her: "Do you want me to fail?" he asks her. But her grandmother shares an interesting piece of family history: her uncle Rawiri—who is now mired in idleness and squalor by a drug addiction—was once a champion of this ritual fighting ("before he was fat and ugly," she comments). So she suggests that Paikea ask him for private lessons. Rawiri's friends and girlfriend are surprised to learn that as a young boy he was once a master of ancient traditions; and indeed, Rawiri has really forgotten this about himself—a microcosmic picture of the way he has generally forgotten who he was (and is). But when Paikea invites him to train her, as soon as he grabs the staff, there is a transformation. This artifact of the tradition has an almost sacramental character and seems to immediately recall him to himself, to remind him of not only who he was but who he is called to be. This reacquaintance with the tradition has a remarkably humanizing effect on one from the lost generation. Rawiri takes up the challenge with fervor and not only trains Paikea to be the best in the tribe but also recovers his own sense of identity and worth.[2]

Koro's sacred school of firstborns is finally subjected to one last test to discern which is the One destined to bring the charism of chief back to the tribe. Koro takes the boys out into the bay in a rickety aluminum boat (which is a small, ugly artifact of modernity compared with the massive decorated hull of the *waka* they can see on shore the whole time). Anchoring in a deep section of the bay, he removes from his neck a whale-tooth amulet (a *reiputa*) and throws it into the deep: "One of you will bring it back to me," he announces. The boys dive into the water, eager to retrieve the whale's tooth and seal their identity as chief-in-waiting. One by one they bob up to the surface, until Koro finally asks, "Well, which one of you has it?" None could retrieve the amulet. They return to shore in silence; Koro makes his way to his bed and remains there for days on end. He has failed; the ancestors have ignored his prayers; his people are doomed to the darkness of forgetting.

But Paikea has heard her grandfather's prayers and sympathizes with his struggles. "He was calling to the ancient ones," she tells us in a voice-over, "asking them to help him. But they weren't listening. . . . So I tried." She makes her way out to the empty, haunting hull of the *waka*. It is into the skeleton-like presence of the *waka* that Paikea retreats when she feels her grandfather's rejection most intensely. It was also the site of an important conversation with her father, when he briefly returned to the tribe. At that time Paikea was intensely aware of Koro's rejection, and

2. This positive impact of the tradition is seen in another episode related to the sacred school. One of the sharpest young boys, Hemi (clearly one that Koro has his hopes set on to be the One), is the son of an absentee, wayward father who is also part of this lost generation, sucked in by the wiles of modern culture. But when he briefly visits the *marae* to see Hemi's ritual performance, he swells with pride—even though he immediately leaves the *marae*, as if to protect himself from this pull of the ancestors. But by the end of the film he cannot withstand this pull; he is one of the decorated tribesmen who launches the *waka*. Then Hemi beams in pride at his father.

Porourangi had explained to her: "He's looking for something that doesn't exist anymore." He's looking for a "prophet," someone to "lead [their] people out of the darkness."

But at this time Paikea retreats to the *waka* to pray for her grandfather—to call the ancestors in his stead. "And they heard me." This initiates the transformative sequence of the film: one night Paikea gives her award-winning speech in "love and respect" for her grandfather, in which she explains the story of her people and tearfully recognizes that she was not the leader that her grandfather expected; on this same night, Paka finally emerges from his room and is about to attend Paikea's speech but is turned back to the beach. Distant cries lure him to the shore, where he finds an entire pod of whales have beached themselves and are slowly dying. "Who's to blame?" he asks himself. The ancestors had heard Paikea's prayers and tears, and had come. But what did it mean? "It was a test," Paikea concludes.

The entire tribe comes together in the face of this tragedy and labors through the night to try to save the whales. They drape the creatures with dampened blankets and run to and from the sea with pails of water. When one of the whales dies in the hour before dawn, Rawiri comforts a grief-stricken woman who, just hours before, was one of the cynical old women gathered around the card table. The death of the whale has sparked in her a memory of a way of life she has forgotten. But their nocturnal labors for the whales is tinged with futility as the sun begins to rise: further down the beach they see the massive hulk of a whale that must be ancient, dwarfing those they have been tending. If it has seemed almost hopeless to get these smaller creatures back in the water, what is the hope for saving this mammoth?

Koro approaches the gentle, colossal creature with chants and prayers and quickly diagnoses the situation: they need to find some way to turn the animal around and get it headed back out to sea. Then the others will follow. He barks at Rawiri to gather everyone for this task, but Rawiri is less confident: they've been working all night, he replies. "They'll do it for you," Koro responds—a first indication that Koro sees in his second-born the charism of a leader. Rawiri gathers together the tribe to devote themselves to this Herculean, impossible task. The strategy seems simple: attaching a massive rope to the tail, which will be pulled with a tractor, both men and women will push simultaneously on the head and attempt to redirect the whale. The tractor strains and the rope begins to fray, eventually snapping.[3] What now? Is there any hope?

Paikea has been watching all this from the hull of the *waka*. After the tribe leaves the shore, she makes her way down to the water's edge and inches cautiously toward the whale. Mimicking the traditional Maori greeting she has known since she was a child, Paikea rubs noses with the whale, prayerfully, trying to discern what she ought to do. Slowly, but resolutely, she climbs up on the back of the animal and assumes the stance of her namesake: Paikea the ancient whale rider. The whale responds to her entreaties, beats its tail fin against the sand, and begins to maneuver its massive body toward the ocean's depths. Paikea remains on the whale's back, riding the creature as it leads the other beached whales back to the depths, where they can flourish. Paikea seems to refuse to let go and remains attached to the whale as it makes its descent into the water.

As this is happening, Paikea's grandmother begins to search for her: "Where is she? Where is she?" the grandmother cries. This turns the tribe's attention to the beach and to the ocean, where they see the young Paikea riding the whale back out to sea. With tears of sadness and anger, the grandmother puts something into Koro's hand: the whale's tooth none of the boys had been able to retrieve. "Which one?" he asks.

"What do you mean 'which one?'" his wife replies, indignantly. Koro knows.

The force of the dive pushes Paikea off the whale's back, and she is later retrieved from the waters, in serious condition. Koro cautiously enters her hospital room, humbles himself before young Paikea, kneeling beside her in submission: "Forgive me, O Wise Leader. I am just a fledgling new to flight." The scene

---

3. This recalls an earlier incident in the film: Paikea is with her Paka as he works on the pull cord of a battered old outboard engine. Paikea's curiosity about the tribe's myth leads her to ask about their connection to the ancestors. Paka responds by using the analogy of the rope in his hands: Their heritage is like this rope, he suggests, which is made up of many tiny strands. So, too, they are part of a long line of chiefs that is made up of many ancestors. When Koro then uses the rope to start the motor, it snaps. As he goes to retrieve another cord, Paikea repairs the rope and starts the engine. "I don't want you to do that again," Paka scolds her. "It's dangerous."

then cuts to the underwater serenity of a young whale playfully dancing underneath its mother. Koro has found the charism of the ancestors where he had least expected it.

In the closing scene of the film, we see that the creative, unexpected retrieval of the tradition led by Paikea has transformed and renewed the community: cutting across a shot of blue sky is the bow of the *waka*, now completed and shimmering in bright colors, its intricate carving completed by Porourangi, who has returned home. He and Rawiri lead the team of those from the lost generation as they roll the *waka* out to sea and launch it on its maiden voyage. On the shore are groups of tribal dancers in traditional costume and paint, chanting and singing according to the old ways and led by some of the young men and women who had been mired in drugs and the underside of modernity. While the film does not present a simplistic rejection of modernity (modern medicine nurses Paikea back to health), it is the recovery of tradition *in* modernity, and sometimes against modernity, that makes possible the renewal of the identity of Paikea's people. It is the strangeness of ancient ritual and the outlandish notion of whale riding that grants them a future.

Redeeming Dogma: A More Persistent Postmodernism

The church would do well by learning to ride whales. We need to be attentive and discerning about the way modernity has eroded our identity as the "peculiar people" who make up the body of Christ and seek to retrieve the strange ways and ancient practices of the communion of the saints in order to re-form who we are. In this concluding chapter, we will see that the outcome of the postmodernism sketched in earlier chapters should be a robust confessional theology and ecclesiology that unapologetically reclaims premodern practices in and for a postmodern culture. A more persistent postmodernism—one that really follows through on the implications of claims made by Derrida, Lyotard, and Foucault (or better, the meshing of their central claims with insights from the Christian theological tradition)—will issue not in a thinned-out, sanctified version of religious skepticism (a "religion without religion") offered in the name of humility and compassion but rather should be the ground for the proclamation and adoption of "thick" confessional identities. Much that we find in the name of postmodern spirituality, or even in the name of an "emerging" Christianity, is a timidity with respect to the particularities of the Christian confessional tradition. While this is almost certainly a corrective with respect to rabid forms of fundamentalism—whether Protestant or Catholic—a retreat into a thinly "ecumenical" Christianity that reduces confession to bland concerns with justice or love still remains a latent version of a very modern project.[4] In this respect much of the dominant discussion in postmodern theology or philosophy of religion actually shrinks back from the more radical implications of the postmodern critique.

The most persistent postmodernism will issue in a postmodern dogmatics—or what we might call a postcritical dogmatics of second naiveté. And on the level of practice, a more persistent postmodernism will engender not quite a postmodern church but rather a postmodern catalyst for the church to *be* the church.

In this respect a recent movement or sensibility in Christian theology embodies this more persistent postmodernism. Radical Orthodoxy[5]—a sensibility that seeks to articulate a robust confessional theology in postmodernity—represents a more persistent or thoroughgoing postmodernism insofar as it refuses the modern (and skeptical) equation of knowledge with omniscience. In other words, unlike much postmodern theology or Continental philosophy of religion, Radical Orthodoxy refuses to be haunted by Cartesian anxiety.[6]

What do we mean by this? We must appreciate the sense in which many advocates of postmodern theology or religion are

4. For my criticism of Derrida on this point, see James K. A. Smith, "Re-Kanting Postmodernism: Derrida's Religion within the Limits of Reason Alone," *Faith and Philosophy* 17 (2000): 558–71.

5. For a more extensive introduction, including a consideration of Radical Orthodoxy's relation to other like movements (e.g., postliberalism), see James K. A. Smith, *Introducing Radical Orthodoxy: Mapping a Post-secular Theology* (Grand Rapids: Baker, 2004).

6. For a helpful discussion of the long shadow cast over theology by Descartes' doubt, see Nancey Murphy and Brad J. Kallenberg, "Anglo-American Postmodernity: A Theology of Communal Practice," in *The Cambridge Companion to Postmodern Theology*, ed. Kevin Vanhoozer (Cambridge: Cambridge University Press, 2003), 26–41. As they point out, a properly postmodern theology will refuse the terms of the debate set by Descartes at the origins of modernity.

deeply critical of particular, determinate formulations of religious confession. Figures such as Derrida and John D. Caputo rightly point out (and many who are part of the emergent conversation are very sympathetic on this score) that the modern Cartesian dream of absolute certainty is just that: a dream, and, admittedly, one that has been a nightmare for those who have become victims to such rational confidence (colonized peoples, an exploited creation, etc.). And far too often, some version of Cartesian certainty has attached itself to particular religious expressions—the result is what we call fundamentalism—and engendered untold harm. The problem with such modern religion—whether in the form of post-Kantian liberal theology or the equally modernist versions of Protestant fundamentalism—is twofold: on the one hand, it rests on a mythical epistemology of immediate access and cognitive certainty; on the other hand, its fruit has included harm, violence, and suffering for communities, both to those within such communities and to those regarded as "other" by these religious communities.

If, then, we are going to be *post*modern—if we are going to get rid of what is worst about modernity—then surely we need to abandon not only foundationalist epistemology but also the forms of religion that have hitched their wagon to this Cartesian train. But for Derrida, Caputo, and others, the rejection of modernist religion (and its attendant epistemology) takes the form of a critique that might be said to still accept the rules of the game laid down by Descartes. In particular, a common move in postmodern theology[7] is to reject the Cartesian equation of knowledge with quasi-omniscient certainty, instead asserting a kind of radical skepticism that opposes faith to knowledge but thereby actually retains the Cartesian equation of knowledge and certainty. "I don't *know*," Derrida once said; "I must *believe*."[8] In other words, the postmodern theologian says, "We can't *know*

7. "Theology" is not quite the right term here, and Caputo and Derrida would be somewhat uncomfortable with the term, since it seems to have too much a sense of being linked to a determinate confession. Instead, they would describe this as "postmodern philosophy of religion" or simply "religious studies." My employment of the term "theology" in this context is largely heuristic and a shorthand.

8. See Jacques Derrida, *Memoirs of the Blind*, trans. Pascale-Anne Brault and Michel Naas (Chicago: University of Chicago Press, 1993), 155.

that God was in Christ reconciling the world to himself. The best we can do is *believe.*" Why? Because to know would mean being certain. We know that such certainty is an impossible dream; therefore, we actually lack knowledge. We don't know; we can only believe, and such faith will always be mysterious and ambiguous. But this isn't a bad thing; quite to the contrary, it is liberating and just. It is precisely when we think we know something about God that we start erecting boundaries and instituting discipline. People who *know* what God wants effect the worst sort of violence on those who don't know, even on those who are part of the "knowing" community. Not only infidels are harmed by such "believers" (who are really "knowers") but also those internal to the religious community, who are subjected to all kinds of legalistic rules, even if they are self-imposed. So postmodern religious faith eschews knowledge and therefore also eschews the particularity of dogma and doctrine. In other words, according to this line of thinking, postmodern faith sees any particular, determinate religious confession as still tainted by knowledge; instead, the postmodernist advocates a "religion without religion" that is not linked to any particular creed or denomination—a more transcendent, less determinate (or even indeterminate) commitment to justice or "love."[9]

Much in this critique has been rightly affirmed by many who have tried to think through the shape of the emerging church in postmodernity. Those whose Christian experience has been shaped by American fundamentalism (like myself) are particularly open and receptive to this critique of determinate modern religion since we have seen and experienced firsthand the kind of harm that is done—both to people and the gospel—by such practices and theological formulations. So it is understandable that the emergent church has flirted with a religion without religion, sympathetic to versions of postmodern spirituality that undercut the role of dogma and the institutional church.[10] However, I suggest that such a religion without religion is not really postmodern:

9. For a lucid, entertaining articulation of such a postmodern "religion without religion," see John D. Caputo, *On Religion* (London: Routledge, 2001).

10. It is this aspect of the emerging church that D. A. Carson criticizes so harshly regarding questions of truth and objective knowledge. But as I noted in chapter 2, I am trying to sketch a third way between radical, albeit religious, skepticism and Carson's confidence in objectivity. This third, Augustinian way

it is rather an extension of deeply modern sensibilities. Further, a more properly postmodern theology will reject the very terms of this critique and, in fact, be much more hospitable to both dogmatic theology and the institutional church.

First, this quasi-postmodern religion without religion does not upset the modern Cartesian formulation of the problem. Instead, it proceeds by accepting the Cartesian equation of knowledge with certainty; then, because such certainty is impossible, it must conclude that knowledge is impossible. But we need not accept this all-or-nothing logic. Indeed, before Descartes this would have seemed simply mistaken. From Augustine through Aquinas, medieval theologians were very attentive to the difference between "comprehending" God (which was impossible) and "knowing" God (which was possible, because God had given himself to us in terms that could be received).[11] Why should we think that the criterion for knowledge is godlike certainty or omniscience? Why should we accept the clearly mistaken modern equation of the two? Quasi-postmodern religion without religion actually accepts and works from this Cartesian paradigm, whereas a more persistent or proper postmodernism rejects this paradigm as an aberration in the history of philosophy and theology.[12]

It is precisely this refusal of the Cartesian paradigm that characterizes Radical Orthodoxy, which seeks to reanimate the account of knowledge offered by Augustine and Aquinas. On this ancient-medieval-properly-postmodern model, we rightly give up pretensions to absolute knowledge or certainty, but we do not thereby give up on knowledge altogether. Rather, we can properly confess that we know God was in Christ reconciling the world

---

affirms the possibility and reality of knowledge and truth but rejects the modern notion of objectivity. It is, we might say, a confessional realism.

11. For more on this point, see James K. A. Smith, *Speech and Theology: Language and the Logic of the Incarnation*, Radical Orthodoxy Series (London: Routledge, 2002), chap. 5.

12. Murphy and Kallenberg note Stephen Toulmin's suggestion that modernity "is a giant Ω-shaped detour" ("Anglo-American Postmodernity," 39, citing Toulmin, *Cosmopolis: The Hidden Agenda of Modernity* [Chicago: University of Chicago Press, 1990], 167). The idea is that the turn made with Descartes has been shown to be a wrong turn, and as we get back on track, we find significant continuity with premodern forebears. This affirms Webber's "ancient-future" thesis and explains the invocation of the epistemologies of Augustine and Aquinas as more properly postmodern.

to himself, but such knowledge rests on the gift of (particular, special) revelation,[13] is not universally objective or demonstrable, and remains a matter of interpretation and perspective (with a significant appreciation for the role of the Spirit's regeneration and illumination as a condition for knowledge). We confess knowledge without certainty, truth without objectivity.

Second, it is the acceptance of the modern Cartesian paradigm that undergirds Derrida's and Caputo's critique of dogma and determinate religious confession. To confess something determinate and embody this in dogma or doctrine would be to claim to know something about the transcendent, and the inverted Cartesian skepticism of this quasi-postmodernism can't have that. Postmodern religion without religion's resulting affirmation of "faith" seems both deeply fideistic and anti-institutional. The most significant problem with this, from a Christian perspective, is that it is deeply unincarnational. It operates with what I have elsewhere described as a "logic of determination" rather than a "logic of incarnation."[14] According to this logic of determination, particularity itself is violent and leads to violence; therefore, in order to avoid violence we must have, for instance, a social hope that is indeterminate and hopes for a justice that is unspecified, or we must have a religious community without dogma or discipline. But Derrida's premise, which equates determination with violence, can and must be called into question. The determinate and finite would be construed as violent and exclusionary only if one assumes that finitude is somehow a failure—implying that we are somehow called to be infinite. In short, to accept Derrida's premise that all determination or finitude constitutes violence, one would have to adopt some version of a gnostic

13. It must be noted that Derrida and Caputo rule out a priori any possibility of a particular, determinate revelation. This is perhaps one of the most fundamental differences with Radical Orthodoxy, which, like Barth, begins from an affirmation of a given, particular revelation of God in Christ. The religion-without-religion paradigm seems to deny the very *possibility* of revelation, whereas postliberalism and Radical Orthodoxy affirm the *primacy* of a given revelation.

14. See James K. A. Smith, "Determined Violence: Derrida's Structural Religion," *Journal of Religion* 78, no. 2 (April 1998): 197–212; and *Speech and Theology*, chap. 5. I will unpack this further in a forthcoming book, the working title of which is *Holy Wars and Democratic Crusades: Deconstructing Myths of Religious Violence and Secular Peace*.

ontology, which construes finitude as a kind of fall, an original violation. But we are free to reject this premise, particularly on Christian grounds.

Instead of adopting a logic of determination that construes finitude or particularity as a violence, I advocate a logic of incarnation that honors finitude and particularity as a good. If one begins, instead, with an affirmation of embodiment as good, then the fact of finitude and particularity—for example, the confession that God became flesh at a particular time ("under Pontius Pilate") and in a particular place ("born of the Virgin Mary")—is not construed as injustice or violence, because with the rejection of Derrida's logic of determination one must also reject the very modern notion of an ahistorical, a-geographical, transcendental religion. Therefore, it follows that the particularity of religious confession is not violent per se. (It can even be argued that one can locate the seeds of such an incarnational logic in undeveloped aspects of Derrida's early work, such that we might be able to deconstruct Derrida on just this point.)[15]

Christian confession begins from the scandalous reality that God became flesh, and became flesh in a particular person, at a particular time, and in a particular place. The affirmation of particularity is at the very heart of the incarnation, which is itself a reaffirmation of the goodness of particularity affirmed at creation. This affirmation of particularity is then extended in and by the body of Christ, which is the church. But such an incarnational affirmation of embodiment and particularity—including the particularities of dogmatic confession, institutional organization, historical unfolding of doctrine, and so on—is more properly postmodern than the lingering modernism of a religion without religion that, in Kantian fashion, reduces faith to a generic affirmation of love or justice. A more persistent postmodernism embraces the incarnational scandal of determinate confession and its institutions: dogmatic theology and a confessionally governed church.[16] Perhaps in its most scandalous

15. See James K. A. Smith, "A Principle of Incarnation in Derrida's (*Theologische?*) *Jugendschriften*: Towards a Confessional Theology" *Modern Theology* 18 (2002): 217–30.

16. To reaffirm our point in chapter 4 in dialogue with Foucault, where we noted that the continued penchant for nondenominational spirituality could be seen as a lingering form of modern autonomy.

form, there is nothing more postmodern than hierarchy![17] (And nothing more modern than autonomous, nondenominational anarchy.)

So far, I have been suggesting that a properly postmodern theology will be dogmatic, not skeptical. This is not to advocate a return to an uncritical fundamentalism or the triumphalist stance of the Religious Right. Rather, it is to affirm that our confession and practice must proceed unapologetically from the particularities of Christian confession as given in God's historical revelation in Christ and as unfolded in the history of the church's response to that revelation. To be dogmatic, then, is to be unapologetically confessional, which requires being unapologetic about the determinate character of our confession, contra the Cartesian anxiety exhibited by much postmodern theology. This should translate into a robust appropriation of the church's language as the paradigm for both thought and practice. While this affirmation of the primacy of revelation is a core tenet of Radical Orthodoxy, it is one shared with other movements in postmodern theology, including postliberalism.[18] But this issue of the primacy of revelation raises another concern I'd like to briefly address before moving to a more specific consideration of what an incarnational affirmation of history entails for worship and discipleship.

One of the concerns I have about the shape of the postmodern or emerging church is what could technically be described as a correlationist model.[19] "Correlation" refers to a theological strategy whose pedigree is distinctly modern. It operates as follows: beginning with a certain confidence in the findings of a secular discipline—whether philosophy, psychology, history, or sociology—a correlationist theology adapts this neutral or scientific framework as a foundation and then correlates Christian theological claims with the facts disclosed by secular science.

17. For some background considerations, see John Milbank, *Theology and Social Theory* (Oxford: Blackwell, 1990), chap. 10.

18. For a lucid introduction to postliberal theology, see George Hunsinger, "Postliberal Theology," in *Cambridge Companion to Postmodern Theology*, 42–57. See also Brian D. McLaren, *A Generous Orthodoxy* (El Cajon, CA: Emergent Youth Specialties; Grand Rapids: Zondervan, 2004), chap. 8.

19. I unpack this model in more detail in *Introducing Radical Orthodoxy*, 33–42.

For instance, Bultmann accepted the neutral (supposed) facts of Heidegger's existential account of the human condition and then correlated Christian theology to fit this model. Or liberation theology took the findings of Marxist sociology as disclosing the scientific facts about human community and then correlated Christian theology with this "scientific" foundation. In every case, correlationist theology has a deeply *apologetic* interest: ultimately, the goal is to make Christianity intelligible or rational to a given culture (even if it operates on the assumption of a transcultural, neutral, objective reason). In the process, however, primacy is given not to the particularity of Christian revelation or the confessional tradition but rather to the poles of science, experience, and so on, which are taken to be neutral "givens."[20]

But such a correlational method is true not only in theology; we can also clearly see it in church practice. In fact, one of the most trenchant critiques of contemporary evangelicalism has charged the church with looking primarily to its surrounding culture for the norms of what it means to be, or better, to "do," church. Thus seeker-sensitive churches have sought to translate or correlate the gospel into terms of a given (usually white, upper-middle-class) culture, even giving a certain priority to this cultural pole. What Robert Webber helpfully describes as "pragmatic evangelicalism"[21] operates on a deeply modernist level. And many in the emerging church have been critical of just this cultural assimilation, which has dominated the megachurch, church-growth paradigm. But I wonder whether, in the name of creating a postmodern church, the emerging church continues this correlation by other means. While this is by no means a monolithic phenomenon, there are certainly streams in emerging discussions that are simply looking to update the church and bring it into correlation with a postmodern rather than a modern culture. Those in the emergent

---

20. A classic representative of correlational theology is David Tracy. See his *Blessed Rage for Order: The New Pluralism in Theology* (Chicago: University of Chicago Press, 1996); and idem, *The Analogical Imagination: Christian Theology and the Culture of Pluralism* (New York: Herder & Herder, 1998). The same correlational method lies, I would suggest, behind the Wesleyan quadrilateral (which appeals to Scripture, tradition, reason, and experience as "sources" of theology), which has been widely recovered as of late.

21. Webber, *The Younger Evangelicals: Facing the Challenges of the New World* (Grand Rapids: Baker, 2002), 41.

conversation who are more reflective see this for what it is: more of the same and really just an extension of (modern) pragmatic evangelicalism. However, even among more reflective emergent thinkers, one can see hints of a retained correlational stance. There remains a certain notion that the church needs to "get with" postmodernity such that postmodern culture sets an agenda for the church, rather than postmodernity being a catalyst for the church to recover its own authentic mission.[22]

If we hope to be properly postmodern, then we must intentionally resist this correlational model. And here Radical Orthodoxy is instructive in both its diagnosis and prescription. At the level of diagnosis, Milbank observes that "the pathos of modern theology is its false humility."[23] Conceding its foundations to the conditions of modernity and accepting the notion of a neutral science that must position theological discourse, modern theology had to be apologetic. But "once theology surrenders its claim to be a metadiscourse, it cannot any longer articulate the word of the creator God, but is bound to turn into some oracular voice of some finite idol, such as historical scholarship, humanist psychology, or transcendental philosophy. If theology no longer seeks to position, qualify or criticize other discourses, then it is inevitable that these discourses will position theology."[24] But

22. I suspect that some of this lingering correlationism in the emerging church is at least partly due to a lingering correlationism in one of its theological leaders, Stanley Grenz (*requiescat in pace*). This could be seen in his sympathy for the Wesleyan quadrilateral (i.e., four main sources of religious knowledge: Scripture, reason, tradition, and experience) in *Revisioning Evangelical Theology* (Downers Grove, IL: InterVarsity, 1993), a book to which I owe a great deal. (Brian D. McLaren also appeals to the Wesleyan quadrilateral in *A New Kind of Christian: A Tale of Two Friends on a Spiritual Journey* [San Francisco: Jossey-Bass, 2001], 55.) Grenz was attentive to this concern. For instance, in a recent contribution on ecclesiology, he explicitly rejects what he calls a "sociological foundationalism of community," specifically referring to Milbank's critique (see Stanley Grenz, "Ecclesiology," in *Cambridge Companion to Postmodern Theology*, 258). But his method in earlier works, and even in this same essay, seems to indicate a lingering foundationalism or correlational method. For a discussion along these lines, with a response from Grenz, see Archie Spencer, "Culture, Community and Commitments: Stanley J. Grenz on Theological Method," *Scottish Journal of Theology* 57 (2004): 338–60.

23. John Milbank, *Theology and Social Theory: Beyond Secular Reason* (Oxford: Blackwell, 1990), 1.

24. Ibid.

it is precisely the postmodern critique of Derrida, Lyotard, and Foucault that has unmasked this myth of a neutral scientific discourse that could position the supposed irrationality of theological discourse. All discourses and disciplines proceed from commitments and beliefs that are ultimately religious in nature. No scientific discourse (whether natural science or social science) simply discloses to us the facts of reality to which theology must submit; rather, every discourse is, in some sense, religious. The playing field has been leveled. Theology is most persistently postmodern when it rejects a lingering correlational false humility and instead speaks unapologetically from the primacy of Christian revelation and the church's confessional language. Radical Orthodoxy, then, is more properly postmodern than Derridean religious skepticism precisely because it embraces this situation. Indeed, it is "intended to overcome the pathos of modern theology, and to restore in postmodern terms, the possibility of theology as a metadiscourse."[25]

The rejection of correlation with respect to theology should also be true of our understanding of church practice, worship, and discipleship. If the pathos of modern theology is its false humility, it might be that the persistent pathos of postmodern Christian practice and the emerging church is a continued false humility. If Christian theology should proceed from the primacy of God's revelation in Christ and Scripture, then Christian practices of worship and discipleship should do the same. Our understanding of what it means to be the church must be shaped by the priority of revelation and the Christian tradition, not what (even) a postmodern culture needs or is looking for. A radically orthodox church practice will refuse the correlational idol of relevance without giving up the central impetus of hospitality. We see this modeled in the case of *Whale Rider*: the community's capitulation to modernity only spelled disaster. Rejection of tradition in favor of modernity showed itself to be a failure. But the solution was not to broker a compromise with modernity either—to come up with a correlation between modernity's tenets and a thinned-out version of the faith tradition that was "suitable" for moderns. (Correlation always privileges the culture, whether of modernity or postmodernity.) Rather, healing and

25. Ibid.

communal wholeness were found when the community risked putting its tradition first—when it granted primacy to its faith stories and let those stories position their response to and appropriation of modernity (or postmodernity).[26] This was not a simple going backward either: it was a nonidentical repetition of the tradition in a postmodern context. It was not a nostalgic, romantic return to old paths. This was a creative retrieval of the tradition *for* a postmodern culture. After all, the charism of chief was unexpectedly incarnated in a girl.

Recovering Tradition: Taking History Seriously

I have suggested that a more persistent postmodernism, articulated by Radical Orthodoxy, begins from a primary affirmation of the incarnation. In the preceding section I argued that if our theology and practice are going to be fundamentally incarnational, then they should be the catalysts for a reaffirmation of the particularities of Christian dogma, confession, and ecclesial practice. I want to extend this incarnational logic into two more spheres that are significant for Christian worship and discipleship in the postmodern world. First, in this section, I suggest that the incarnation should entail a deep affirmation of time and history, which should translate into church practice that is catholic and traditional (though in a postmodern mode). The following section explores the implications of the incarnational affirmation of space along two axes: an affirmation of liturgy and the arts and a commitment to place and local communities.

Let us first think about time. There is a significant sense in which modernity tried to transcend time in its quest for universal, ahistorical principles and truths that applied at all times, in all places, to all people. This universal penchant for ahistoricality resulted in the colonial imposition of one particular set of practices as rational and universal, when in fact they were the fruit of a very determinate history and geography. In this respect modernity represented a revival of traditional Platonism, which held that ideas—and it is ideas that modernity really cared

26. This might be embodied in the way that modern technology and tools could be appropriated to complete and launch the *waka* (war canoe). What mattered was the identity that was wrapped up in the *waka*.

about—trafficked in the eternal, unchanging, atemporal realm of the Forms.[27] In other words, to grasp an idea was to transcend time, and the ideas that really mattered were not conditioned by time or change. In fact, it was the realm of bodies and matter—the realm of generation and decay—that was also the realm of time, history, and change. Thus it is no surprise that modernity, launched by the disembodied Cartesian "thinking thing," would come to have an ambivalent relationship to the world of bodies and time. History, rather than being affirmed as the arena for the material unfolding of latent possibilities, was something to be subdued and transcended. For Kant, for instance, what was properly ethical or good could not bear any relationship to the particular contingencies of time or place.

The church's theology bought into this ahistoricism in different ways: along a more liberal, post-Kantian trajectory, the historical particularities of Christian faith were reduced to atemporal moral teachings that were universal and unconditioned. Thus it turned out that what Jesus taught was something like Kant's categorical imperative—a universal ethics based on reason rather than a set of concrete practices related to a specific community. Liberal Christianity fostered ahistoricism by reducing Christianity to a universal, rational kernel of moral teaching. Along a more conservative, evangelical trajectory (and the Reformation is not wholly innocent here), it was recognized that Christians could not simply jettison the historical particularities of the Christian event: the birth, life, death, and resurrection of Jesus Christ. However, there was still a quasi-Platonic, quasi-gnostic rejection of material history such that evangelicalism, while not devolving to a pure ahistoricism, became dominated by a modified ahistoricism we can call primitivism. Primitivism retains the most minimal commitment to God's action in history (in the life

27. I should clarify that my reference to "Platonism" here is to a traditional understanding of Plato as a dualist. In fact, Radical Orthodoxy seeks to retrieve quite a different Plato in a positive, non-dualistic way. Though I criticize the dualism or "Platonism" of modern Christianity here, I don't mean to suggest that Radical Orthodoxy is critical of Platonism per se. For a discussion of the issues, see my chapter, "Will the Real Plato Please Stand Up? Participation versus Incarnation," in *Radical Orthodoxy and the Reformed Tradition*, ed. James K. A. Smith and James H. Olthuis (Grand Rapids: Baker, 2005), 61–72. My thanks to Geoff Holsclaw for noting this tension.

of Christ and usually in the first century of apostolic activity)[28] and then seeks to make only this first-century "New Testament church" normative for contemporary practice.[29] This is usually articulated by a rigid distinction between Scripture and tradition (the latter then usually castigated as "the traditions of men" as opposed to the "God-given" realities of Scripture).[30] Such primitivism is thus anticreedal and anticatholic, rejecting any sense that what was unfolded by the church between the first and the twenty-first centuries is at all normative for current faith and practice (the question of the canon's formation being an interesting exception here). Ecumencial creeds and confessions—such as the Apostles' Creed or the Nicene Creed—that unite the church across time and around the globe are not "live" in primitivist worship practices, which enforce a sense of autonomy or even isolation, while at the same time claiming a direct connection to first-century apostolic practices.[31]

I'm suggesting that this anticatholic ahistoricism stems from the absorption of a modern aversion to the logic of incarnation and the affirmation of the goodness of creation—and the attendant affirmation of embodiment, change, time, history, and therefore tradition. To affirm the goodness of creation[32] (Gen.

28. The fact that primitivists accept the shape of the biblical canon as determined several centuries later is a nasty little exception to this rule.

29. This might be most radically played out in Plymouth Brethren traditions (the tradition of my own conversion to Christian faith), but this stance is quintessentially Baptist. However, Pentecostal Christianity tends to operate on the same principle. It is not a coincidence that all these streams emphasize the autonomy of the local congregation.

30. For a lucid critique of this framework from a card-carrying evangelical, see F. F. Bruce, "Scripture and Tradition in the New Testament," in *Holy Book and Holy Tradition*, ed. F. F. Bruce and E. G. Rupp (Manchester: Manchester University Press, 1968), where Bruce argues that the New Testament itself constitutes an interpretive tradition.

31. This primitivism opens up such evangelical traditions to any new wind of doctrine. The key is for such new doctrines to assert their first-century, primitive origins. So, for instance, the radically novel eschatology of dispensationalism could become the dominant orthodoxy in just half a century because it claimed biblical rather than traditional warrant. For a relevant discussion, see Larry V. Crutchfield, *The Origins of Dispensationalism: The Darby Factor* (Lanham, MD: University Press of America, 1992).

32. The incarnation is a reaffirmation of the goodness of both time and space.

1:31) is to affirm the goodness of time, time's unfolding in history, and the fruit of this process in tradition. As John Milbank puts it, it is not just the material creation that "participates" in God; our own human *poiēsis*, or "making," is a kind of co-creation that also participates in God's transcendence. In other words, human cultural making—including the culture making of the church's institutions and practices over time—is an arena of the Spirit's continued activity and revelation.[33]

While the emerging church rightly rejects the disincarnate theologies and practices of pragmatic evangelicalism, I wonder if it has retained something of modernity's ahistoricism or its evangelical version, primitivism. In the name of postmodern Christianity, we often hear sentiments about believing in Jesus but not Christianity, not letting tradition distort Jesus's radical message in the Gospels, or sorting out the nonnegotiable essentials of the gospel from traditions—where, ironically, the traditions in question are usually the machinations of pragmatic evangelicalism. Sometimes this is expressed in a regulative principle about theological concepts: if a theological concept isn't in the Bible, then it lacks any normativity.[34] This also underwrites a persistent non- or even antidenominationalism in the emerging church, which rejects the normative confessional boundaries of any institutional hierarchies. This relates to our earlier observation of a lingering affirmation of autonomy in the emerging church; along the axis of time, we see a lingering, disincarnate rejection of time, history, and tradition.

Radical Orthodoxy articulates an incarnational affirmation of history that could help the emerging church think through its

33. As Milbank stipulates, "I have always tried to suggest that participation can be extended also to language, history and culture: the whole realm of human *making*. Not only do being and knowledge participate in a God who is and who comprehends; also human making participates in a God who is infinite poetic utterance: the second person of the Trinity" (John Milbank, *Being Reconciled* [London: Routledge, 2003], ix).

34. For instance, despite McLaren's healthy affirmation of tradition in *A Generous Orthodoxy* (El Cajon, CA: Emergent Youth Specialties; Grand Rapids: Zondervan, 2004), 87, he often makes such observations as the following: "For much of Western Christianity, the doctrine of creation (a biblical term) has been eaten alive by the doctrine of the fall (not a biblical term)" (234). I understand the distinction, but a thoroughgoing incarnational theology will think the distinction a moot point.

commitment to the incarnation by exorcising its latent primitivism. For, as Catherine Pickstock announces, "one of the most central aims of a radically orthodox perspective is to restore time and embodiment to our understanding of reality."[35] On this more incarnational account, time is not "something to be lamented or circumvented by means of the instruments of nostalgia, but rather as our very condition of possibility *per se*."[36] If we are created as finite, temporal creatures, then time is part of the good creational air that we breathe, so to speak. "Changefulness in time is actually what defines us."[37] To be human is to be temporal; to be temporal is to be traditioned, which is simply to say that we are always and only temporal in a social or communal manner.[38]

But this is not a traditional*ism*; an affirmation of time, history, and tradition rejects the notion of a reified, static past that feeds the nostalgia of traditionalism. Rather, Pickstock emphasizes an ancient-future affirmation of time. We are constituted "as much by the past as by the future. For no co-ordinate of time—past, present, or future—wields supreme sway."[39] This "peculiar relationship to time," she concludes, "distances us from both liberals and conservatives, for both these latter tend to invoke theology or the notion of God to underwrite some pre-existing value—whether, for conservatives, some fetish of tradition, or for liberals, some timeless humanist value. Against such positions, [Radical Orthodoxy] would prefer to emphasize that there are no such pre-established givens, for everything is a never-finished work, which yet discloses what lies invisibly within the interstices of time."[40] What is wrong with modernity is its suppression of time, and this suppression of time is seen in both liberal ahistoricism and the conservative evangelical version of ahistoricism: primitivism. In contrast to both, Radical

---

35. Pickstock, "Radical Orthodoxy and the Mediations of Time," in *Radical Orthodoxy? A Catholic Enquiry*, ed. Laurence Paul Hemming (Aldershot: Ashgate, 2000), 64.
36. Ibid.
37. Ibid.
38. For more on traditionality as an essential aspect of creaturehood, see James K. A. Smith, *The Fall of Interpretation: Philosophical Foundations for a Creational Hermeneutic* (Downers Grove, IL: InterVarsity, 2000), 152–57.
39. Pickstock, "Radical Orthodoxy and the Mediations of Time," 64.
40. Ibid., 65.

Orthodoxy asserts an affirmation of time as the incarnate arena for the Spirit's unfolding and thus takes seriously the fruits of time as it becomes embodied in tradition. This is not to make a fetish of tradition but rather to recognize that time is a medium for God's continued revelation and to concede a certain authority and normativity to what precedes us.

The shorthand to describe this affirmation of time and tradition is simple: this is catholic faith. In order for the church to be postmodern, it should be catholic. This might seem counterintuitive at first. But what the emerging church is reacting against is a deep, hurtful experience of sectarianism; the antidote to this is a generous orthodoxy and healthy catholicity. To be emergent should entail being catholic.

It is no secret that the evangelical tradition can take shape in forms that are deeply sectarian, provincial, and polemical.[41] But when we diagnose the cause of such instantiations of evangelical faith, we find one common cause: memory loss. In particular, such sectarian versions of evangelical identity tend to see themselves as relatively new inventions, or—following the logic of primitivism that we've already noted—new recoveries of the "true" faith and "New Testament church principles." The most polemical and schismatic permutations of evangelical faith and practice tend to exhibit a paradoxical blend of primitivism and temporal hubris: on the one hand, they tend to have an air of having just dropped from the sky, but, on the other hand, they claim to give us the only authentic version of Pauline Christianity. While trumpeting notions of recovering the truth, these polemical elements of the evangelical tradition seem to be characterized by a deep forgetting. We might suggest that these versions of Christianity are more interested in being "holy" and "apostolic" than in being "catholic"—as if these traits could be separated.

Much earlier, in the early fifth century, Augustine grappled with another version of sectarianism—Donatism—which also tended to suffer from memory loss. And thus, when pastorally addressing the challenge for his parishioners, Augustine advocated

41. For a comprehensive, and disturbing, account of this in the twentieth-century American Reformed tradition, see John M. Frame, "Machen's Warrior Children," in *Alister E. McGrath and Evangelical Theology: A Dynamic Engagement*, ed. Sung Wook Chung (Carlisle: Paternoster; Grand Rapids: Baker, 2003), 113–46.

remembering. In particular, he charged them: "Remember, you are catholic" (Sermon 52). The emerging church could heed the same admonition today. With Augustine's admonition in mind, the emerging church might find a resource in an unlikely place: papal biographer George Weigel's *Letters to a Young Catholic*.

That an admonition to be catholic would give evangelicals pause is evidence of precisely why such an exhortation is so important. (I've been in evangelical congregations that, if they recite the creed, project it on a screen and expect us to confess "the holy universal church," just to keep things straight.) In an era when even confessional churches are being co-opted by a kind of generic evangelical pragmatism, American civic theology, or mainstream liberalism, Weigel's *Letters* should be received as a reminder of the Augustinian challenge to remember our catholicity. Such a remembering of who we are—disciples of Jesus who are members of one, holy, catholic, apostolic church—is a powerful antidote to both the schismatic and the polemical elements of the evangelical tradition and should also revitalize a sense of *antithesis*, or what Weigel describes as "the catholic difference."[42]

It will be most difficult for evangelicals—particularly "emerging" evangelicals—to imagine themselves as recipients of these letters. Because of various shifts in identity and historical factors, we might not immediately think of ourselves as the audience for a book addressed to "catholics"; but insofar as our credo includes the confession of one holy catholic church, what Weigel articulates is the core of Christian faith and practice. While we often hear the term "catholic" as a way of marking off a body of Christians from other Christians, when Weigel speaks of "the catholic faith," he means the faith that distinguishes the people of God from the secular and pagan faiths of the contemporary world. If there is a polemics here, it is directed not against other Christians (Weigel is not out to demonize Protestants) but against the Christian faith's most seductive foes: secularism, naturalism, and liberalism. When Weigel articulates "the catholic difference," he is not marking off Roman Catholics from Presbyterians but rather describing what distinguishes the people of God as

---

42. George Weigel, *Letters to a Young Catholic* (New York: Basic Books, 2004), 9.

a peculiar people and a holy nation. Indeed, Weigel even wants
to reinvigorate the notion of the ghetto, recalling the Catholic
ghetto of his Baltimore youth: "The most ghettoized people of
all," he concludes, "are those who don't know they grew up in a
particular time and place and culture, and who think they can
get to universal truths outside particular realities and communities."[43] In the same way that some of my Dutch friends are drawn
to the accounts of Hasidic communities in Chaim Potok's fiction,
Weigel gives us a sense in which a community constituted by "the
catholic difference" functions as an empowering ghetto—though
with its own set of struggles and challenges. "The real question,"
he offers, "is not whether you grow up in a ghetto, but whether
the ideas and customs and rhythms of your particular ghetto
prepare you to engage other ideas and customs and life experiences without losing touch with your roots."[44]

Of course, the same peculiar people that are marked by "the
catholic difference" also comprise a transnational and enduring community. So Weigel's strategy for introducing his young
interlocutor to the catholic faith is via a world tour of catholic
places inhabited by exemplars of catholic faith. Beginning with
the Baltimore ghetto of his youth, Weigel takes us on "an epis-
tolary tour" of places such as Saint Peter's Rome, Chesterton's
pub in London, Saint Catherine's Monastery on Mount Sinai, the
Oratory that was home to Cardinal Newman in Birmingham, and
the Basilica of the Holy Trinity in Kraków, one of several Polish
sites in the book. (Curiously absent from the tour are any sites
outside the Northern Hemisphere; indeed, the entire continents
of South America and Africa are silent in this account.) The
result is a rich sketch of the core themes and affirmations that
constitute "the catholic difference," which is, "at bottom, a way
of seeing the world."[45] If you'll permit a Kuyperian indulgence,
I take Weigel to be providing a lucid account of the Christian
world- and life-view. And indeed, the reason I think this book
is such a wonderful reminder of our catholicity—why I receive
it as an Augustinian injunction to remember I am catholic—is
because Weigel helps to locate key themes we traditionally re-

43. Ibid.
44. Ibid.
45. Ibid.

gard as part of a Reformed worldview as ultimately *catholic* Christianity. "While Catholicism is a body of beliefs and a way of life," he remarks, *"Catholicism is also an optic, a way of seeing things, a distinctive perception of reality."*[46] And one of the core features of the optic of Catholicism is its emphasis on tradition. Catholic faith constitutes a community of memory that resists both romanticism and the kind of temporal hubris that dismisses everything prior to 1968. "Christian thinking," Weigel suggests, "should adopt an *ecumenism of time*, employing wisdom and insight from any historical era."[47] In other words, Catholicism is what Chesterton called "a democracy of the dead" because it affirms tradition, which "means giving votes to the most obscure of all classes, our ancestors."[48] It is precisely this ecumenism of time that makes catholic Christianity critical of what Newman described as liberalism in religion.[49] In an era when what we are getting in the name of postmodern spirituality might be more akin to "liberalism," Newman's voice and critique could be an ally in recovering the more antithetical side of the confessional tradition—what Weigel has been calling "the catholic *difference*," or "countercultural Catholicism."

A more persistently postmodern church must be radically incarnational. And to affirm the incarnation is to affirm the scandal of particularity with respect to both space and time. This requires a healthy sense of being constituted by our traditions as we look forward to an eschatological hope in the future. The postmodern church will be a witness to its contemporary generation by being a peculiar people oriented to a coming kingdom through the practices and language of a living tradition.[50] The postmodern church must take the risk of learning to ride whales.

46. Ibid., 10. This way of putting it suggests an overlap with Radical Orthodoxy. Indeed, when showing the way in which Flannery O'Connor's work countered the flatness of "debonair nihilism," Weigel notes: "If Mary McCarthy was right, and the Eucharist only represented Christ in some magical way, then Flannery O'Connor was being utterly, thoroughly, radically orthodox when she muttered, 'Well, if it's a symbol, to hell with it'" (16).

47. Ibid., 80.

48. Ibid., 92.

49. Ibid., Letter 5.

50. On the possibility of speaking ancient languages to a postmodern culture, see Marva Dawn, *Talking the Walk: Letting Christian Language Live Again* (Grand Rapids: Brazos, 2005).

Renewing the Body: Space, Place, and Incarnation

A radical affirmation of the incarnation means affirming not only time (and history and tradition) but also space; that is, it must entail an affirmation of the goodness of the stuff that Descartes described as extended and then wrote off so quickly: bodies, buildings, and bowls of soup. ("Thinking things" never get hungry.) The materiality of God's good creation, like time, is something that modernity sought to repress. And modernist, fundamentalist worship and spirituality reflected this: focused on a didactic sermon meant to convey the ideas that make up the "system" of Christian truth, evangelical worship services have fostered a talking-head Christianity that accords well with the "thinking things" of Cartesian modernity, but not with the robust, fleshy, communal beings that God called into being in Adam and Eve. The iconoclasm and ritual-phobia of evangelical worship bear direct affinity with the disenchanted world bequeathed to us by the immanentism of modern science.

Thus here again, it seems, if we want to be postmodern in some sense, we must recover elements of ancient ritual and practice, for it is liturgy that honors our fleshiness. But this is not a merely traditionalist fiat; it stems from the very way we think about the world and what it means to be human. In other words, an incarnational affirmation of liturgy and the aesthetics of worship is the fruit of an incarnational ontology (an account of the nature of reality) and a holistic anthropology (an account of what it means to be human).[51] If we want to resist the reductionistic Cartesian picture of human persons as "thinking things" (and we should also resist other reductionistic accounts of the human person as merely consuming things or biological things), we must recover the holistic anthropology we find intimated in Scripture and unpacked in the Augustinian catholic tradition. An incarnational anthropology begins with the affirmation that human persons are material: that we don't just inhabit flesh and blood, but we *are* flesh and blood. Being embodied is an essential feature of being a human creature. As such, we are not defined by thinking; rather, we are primarily affective: the center of the person is not

---

51. I unpack this connection in more detail in my *Introducing Radical Orthodoxy*, 223–29.

the mind, but the heart. (That's not to say we are irrational, but only that rationality [mind] is relative to what Augustine calls "the right order of love"—the direction of our heart.) When Pascal famously stated that "the heart has reasons of which reason knows nothing," he meant to assert this primacy of affective, embodied being-in-the-world. This holistic anthropology (or account of the human person) is postmodern precisely because it rejects the reductionism of modernity, but it admittedly recovers key insights of a premodern, biblical worldview.

Because of this fundamental affirmation of embodiment, materiality, and affectivity, a radically orthodox worldview is fundamentally sacramental. It affirms not only the goodness of material bodies but also that the whole realm of the material has a revelational potential. And when this is coupled with the incarnational affirmation of time and tradition, a radically orthodox vision asserts a special mode of sacramentality for aspects of the church's tradition, ritual, and liturgy.

George Weigel gets at the same point when he says that the catholic optic is animated by a *sacramental imagination*. (Once again, I'm suggesting that the best way to be postmodern is to be premodern; to be emergent, one must be catholic.) Weigel sees this sacramental imagination unfolded for us in G. K. Chesterton's old haunt, the Cheshire Cheese pub in London, where we find the rotund apologist enjoying the very material blessings of food and ale. As Weigel puts it, Chesterton's delight in the material world illustrates "the bedrock Catholic conviction that *stuff counts*." Indeed, Weigel makes the radically orthodox claim that only a catholic account of the world can really affirm materiality: "Catholicism takes the world, and the things of the world, far more seriously than those who like to think of themselves as worldly."[52] Both fundamentalists and so-called materialists, he argues, subscribe to a *gnostic imagination*; only those who affirm the paradox of the incarnation can see the world with a sacramental imagination.[53]

We find the same affirmation of stuff in the poetry of Gerald Manley Hopkins and in the almost sacramental (or theurgical)

52. Weigel, *Letters to a Young Catholic*, 86.
53. Ibid., 87, 94.

ladder of love in Evelyn Waugh's *Brideshead Revisited*.[54] And it is ultimately this affirmation of creational stuff that makes us take history seriously, as illustrated in sites of pilgrimage and veneration. In commenting on the *scavi* (excavations) beneath Saint Peter's, Weigel suggests that "the *scavi* and the obelisk—Peter's remains and the last thing Peter may have seen in this life—confront us with the historical tangibility, the sheer grittiness, of Catholicism." The foundations of the Catholic faith are something we can touch.[55]

Although Catholicism may seem to be an otherworldly ideology, Weigel contends that, paradoxically, only catholic faith can really affirm the world—and modern materialists and naturalists actually flatten the world and reduce it to nothingness (and an attendant nihilism). This point is illustrated in what Radical Orthodoxy describes as a "participatory ontology": the sense that we properly understand the nature of the world as creation only when we see that the world "participates" in God. Or, as proponents of this view put it, creation is "suspended" from the divine. The material stuff of the world is "suspended" from the immaterial, invisible God in whom "we live and move and have our being" (Acts 17:28). This suspension of the material is what gives matter its depth, as it were; it makes it more than material. The disenchanted, flattened matter of modern naturalism, on the other hand, actually dissolves matter into nothing. Thus only Christians can be proper materialists!

Because of this Christian materialism, a catholic postmodernism (or postmodern catholicity) affirms sacramentality on two levels. On the one hand, it affirms a general sacramentality: the whole world has potential to function as a window to God and a means of grace from God because God himself affirms materiality as a good thing. We see this not only in creation itself but also in the reaffirmation of it in the incarnation, in which God is happy to inhabit the goodness of flesh. Furthermore, materiality receives an eschatological affirmation in our hope for the resurrection of the body. Even the future kingdom will be a material environment of sacramentality. On the other hand, when an incarnational ontology and anthropology are linked

54. Ibid., 98–100, 101–14.
55. Ibid., 26–27.

with our earlier affirmation of time and tradition, a catholic postmodernism also affirms a special sacramentality—a special presence and means of grace in the sacraments of baptism and Eucharist. Thus a properly postmodern ecclesiology must overcome the triumph of a deeply modernist (and Zwinglian) notion of the ordinances of baptism and communion and recover a thicker, more sacramental practice of worship.

If it seems strange to suggest that only Christians (or what I'm now calling "postmodern catholics") can properly be materialists, a related theme offers a similar reversal of first impressions: despite assumptions that Catholicism is Victorian in its supposed repression of sexuality, in fact at the root of Catholicism is a rich, affirmative theology of the body. Building on the founding affirmation of the incarnation, Weigel provides a kind of exegesis of the Sistine Chapel to help us reach John Paul II's conclusion: that the Sistine Chapel is "the sanctuary of the theology of the human body."[56] The sacramental imagination, which affirms the goodness of creation, animates an iconic imagination that affirms the presence of the invisible in the visible—that "lifts up" the messiness of bodies to be more than biological machines. "Human bodies," Weigel summarizes, "are icons." And if this is pictured in the Sistine Chapel (Letter 8), and undergirds the beauty of Chartres Cathedral as a kind of "antechamber" of heaven (Letter 12), it is articulated most forcefully by John Paul II. "In a move that takes the argument about the sexual revolution as far beyond prudishness as you can imagine, John Paul has proposed that sexual love within the bond of faithful and fruitful marriage is nothing less than an icon of the interior life of God himself."[57] Contrary to the assumptions of the *New York Times* reporter who thought the pope should have been embarrassed by the nudes in the Sistine Chapel, John Paul II steadily sketched a theology of the body in 129 addresses to general audiences between 1979 and 1984. Weigel does an excellent job of showing how countercultural this affirmation of embodiment and sexuality is in our contemporary context.

Taking the incarnation seriously means taking bodies seriously, which means affirming the space that they occupy as an arena of

56. Ibid., 130.
57. Ibid., 131.

revelation and grace. The sacramental imagination begins from the assumption that our discipleship depends not only—not even primarily—on the conveyance of ideas into our minds, but on our immersion in embodied practices and rituals that form us into the kind of people God calls us to be. It is only Cartesian "thinking things" that can do without liturgy; for we embodied creatures, whether ancient or postmodern, the rhythms of ritual and liturgy are gracious practices that enable discipleship and formation. Thus postmodern worship stages a recovery of the aesthetic aspects of the Christian tradition as a crucial means for redirecting our imagination in community—a means for reordering our love.[58] We were created for stories, not propositions; for drama, not bullet points. As someone has suggested, humanity cannot live on prose alone.[59] The story of God-become-flesh is best rendered by the poetry and painting of affective worship rather than the narrowly cognitive didacticism of Power-Pointed "messages." Properly postmodern worship resists such reductionism by reclaiming the holistic, full-orbed materiality of liturgical worship that activates all the senses: hearing (not just "messages" but the poetry of the preached Word), sight (with a renewed appreciation for the visual arts, iconicity, and the architectural space of worship), touch (in communal engagement, but also touching the bread that is Christ's body), taste (the body and blood), and even smell (of wine in the cup of the new covenant but also the fragrance of worship in candles and incense). God's taking on a human body also takes up our bodies into worship and participation in the divine.

Finally, if a radically orthodox, incarnational vision takes time and tradition seriously and affirms the goodness of bodies and space, it should also think carefully about *place*. A radically or-

58. For more on liturgy and sacramentality, including the ontology of participation that undergirds this, see my *Introducing Radical Orthodoxy*, chap. 6.

59. See *Alternative Worship: Resources from and for the Emerging Church*, compiled by Jonny Baker and Doug Gay, with Jenny Brown (Grand Rapids: Baker, 2003), 63. The authors employ Les Murray's distinction between the "narrowspeak" of reductive modernity and the "wholespeak" of a more imaginative worldview, calling for a recovery of wholespeak as the church's language. This "poetic discourse" represents "the re-enchantment or re-mythologization of speech, where speech reflects the Christian imagination, recognizing the importance of symbols, images, 'myths,' and metaphors as well as sharing space and time with music and the visual arts" (ibid.).

thodox vision entails not only a distinct liturgy and aesthetics but also a distinct geography. If modernity fosters an ahistorical penchant for timelessness and a disembodied notion of persons as merely thinking things, it also fosters a disconnection from space and locality. David Matzko McCarthy relates this to the increasing hegemony of the (modern, capitalist) market for which, Marx famously noted, all that is solid melts into air: "Our modern growth economy," he observes, "requires that our attachments to people and things be superficial. We must be on the move in order to follow the market."[60] Not only are we increasingly mobile across national and international territories; we also find that the modern market makes us the kind of people who can't be satisfied in one place for very long. Smaller urban homes can't meet the desire for bigger and better, so we make the market-driven pilgrimage into the suburbs to secure the requisite square footage and adequate number of garage doors (three being the new standard)—even though this also means that we spend increased amounts of time commuting in the solitary space of our SUVs. (Descartes had to retreat into a private room to dream up a "thinking thing"; we have the long drive on I-95 to reinforce this solipsism.)

The suburbs, we might suggest, are quintessentially modern, and so it is not surprising that evangelical churches not only have followed the market but also thrive in "mega" forms in this suburban environment. For instance, the modern facilities of First Family Church in Kansas City include a vast lobby surrounded by plasma-screen TVs, buttressed by a food court, a sprawling Barnes-&-Noble-like bookstore, and entryway to the Christianized version of the magical kingdom for kids (where children are admitted to Sunday school by scanning their bar codes).[61] But perhaps what best signals First Family's dislocation from place is the vast sea of vehicles that surround the church like a metallic moat. Because of this growing distance from the parking lot's edge to the entrance of the gymlike sanctuary (the architecture fosters the iconoclasm of pragmatic evangelicalism),

60. David Matzko McCarthy, *The Good Life: Genuine Christianity for the Middle Class* (Grand Rapids: Brazos, 2004), 42.
61. For a survey of the megachurch phenomenon with a critical eye, see James B. Twitchell, *Branded Nation: The Marketing of Megachurch, College Inc., and Museumworld* (New York: Simon & Schuster, 2004), 47–108.

visitors are greeted by a large golf cart to shuttle primly dressed families into worship. And at the conclusion of worship, parking attendants help direct the rush of SUVs as they head for the exit, dispersing across the suburbs.[62]

The convoy of SUVs making its way to and from "worship" at this suburban congregation owes more to the disembodied, disincarnate worldview of Cartesian modernity than to the radically incarnational confession of the church catholic. Being a properly incarnational, more persistently postmodern church entails not only a sacramental, embodied mode of worship practice but also translates into considerations about the place where we worship. The Christian *ekklēsia* must be not only liturgical but also local; it must transform not only hearts but also neighborhoods; its worship must foster not only discipleship but also justice—indeed, disciples who are passionate about justice.

If the emerging church needs to be catholic, as I've suggested, then it must also recover the notion of parish ministry.[63] The postmodern church must be willing to embrace, above all, those who have been crushed by the underside of modernity: those who inhabit the urban core of our cities. And to do so, it is important that the postmodern church stay put; that is, the church is properly postmodern not when it seeks to "plant" new congregations in the comfortable environs of American suburbia but when it struggles to revitalize existing congregations and communities in our inner cities. (Indeed, I wonder if church "planting" isn't a rather modernist phenomenon, given to an infatuation with the new and wanting to work from a clean slate rather than the

62. Admittedly, the same placelessness and mobility can be true of urban congregations that draw people from long distances—including people who want to worship in "diverse" communities but don't necessarily want to live there. So it is not only suburban churches that fail to enact a "parish" theology committed to place. Simply being located in the core city does not make a congregation a parish. And conversely, it is possible for a suburban church to be actually more properly "parish" oriented. My thanks to Brian McLaren for pushing me on these matters.

63. For an argument along these lines, based on a concrete case study, see Mark Mulder, "A Dissonant Faith: The Exodus of Reformed Dutch Churches from the South Side of Chicago" (Ph.D. diss., University of Wisconsin–Milwaukee, 2003), esp. 141–208, on the interrelation of issues of place and church polity. Mulder advocates recovering a sense of parish as a necessary condition for justice.

messiness of given communities. New construction is always easier than renovation. But there is something about the given- ness and grittiness of existing communities that challenges our autonomous dreams to create or plant the next best thing. And if we can run with the architectural metaphor, I would take a restored Arts and Crafts home from the 1900s over the blandness of new developments any day.)

As Eric Jacobsen suggests, in an era of disincarnate suburban dislocation, incarnational ministry might simply mean praying for sidewalks.[64] Embodied worship must be symbiotically related to the place in which we worship: the neighbor sometimes actu- ally means the one next door. If the Word became flesh and dwelt among us, this should translate into an incarnational geography for the church, countering the disembodied abstraction of moder- nity that has too often been adopted by pragmatic evangelicalism. We need to counter not only the ideas of modernity but also the practices of modernity, and one of its most insidious practices involves a flight from the messy realities of urban community. Sidewalks might represent a threat to Cartesian autonomy, but they can also be a means for the inbreaking of grace.

Taking Radical Orthodoxy to Church

The radically orthodox church, while perhaps not Roman, is nevertheless catholic. And it is precisely this catholicity that takes up the key elements of the churches we toured with Der- rida, Lyotard, and Foucault. In other words, we can see that this unholy trinity of Parisians has unwittingly already pointed us to elements of a more incarnational, even radically orthodox understanding of the church and practice. This is a kind of whale riding: creatively retrieving the empowering core of traditional identity but enacting a rendition of this in and for postmodernity. Such a project is motivated not by nostalgic traditionalism or

---

64. See Eric Jacobsen, *Sidewalks in the Kingdom: New Urbanism and the Christian Faith* (Grand Rapids: Brazos, 2003), 84. Jacobsen provides an excellent introduction to these issues, even if he does not situate the concerns vis-à-vis postmodernism. For more on an incarnational theology of place, see T. J. Gor- ringe, *A Theology of the Built Environment: Justice, Empowerment, Redemption* (Cambridge: Cambridge University Press, 2002).

fear of modernity's eroding effects but rather by an incarnational logic that assumes we are by nature traditioned creatures who properly find our identity only by being traditioned well. Just as Paikea took risks to pray in the tongues of her ancestors, so we must consider that the way forward might run along ancient paths. What we have already affirmed in our earlier tours of postmodern churches—the centrality of the Word, the use of the lectionary, the engagement with the arts, practices as ritual discipline—can now be seen as undergirded by the incarnational affirmation of time (tradition) and space (embodiment).

As we enter the radically orthodox church, we enter a space that is organized by a certain "ergonomics" of community: an eclectic collection of chairs is arranged in concentric circles around a table bearing the sacraments, contained in pottery fashioned by a member of the local parish. This organization of space means that during each phase of worship, members of the congregation are faced by others: they see and are seen by others, which reminds them of the iconic gaze of God, who confronts us in the other (Matt. 25). The worship space is also organized by dynamics of light and darkness: surrealist stained glass casts a colored light over portions of the sanctuary, while candles flicker both light and shadow from chapel stations on the fringes of the sanctuary. Several screens display shifting digital images that function as a kind of digital glass of images drawing us into worship.[65] Like traditional icons—which can be found in one of the side chapels—these digital images function as windows to transcendence. But it is not only the visual arts that draw us into participatory worship. Immediately upon our entering the sanctuary, the scent of burning candles conveys a difference from the concrete jungle we've just emerged from and also distinguishes this experience from the scentless passivity of MTV and film.[66] There is also a curious ambience emitted by an unlikely ensemble playing from one of the chapel stations: a jazz combo with sax, double bass, lead guitar, harmonica, and musical saw.

We are signaled to more intentional worship by an a cappella call to worship in the form of a chant from Afghanistan. This

65. For samples of this kind of visual material, visit sacramentis.com.
66. We also catch a whiff of the scent of good Sumatran (fair-trade) coffee—the new wine of the postmodern church!

draws together the families around the table for the recitation of a poem by one of the congregation's gifted poets. The eclectic ensemble then leads us in worship in song, drawing on hymns of the faith, choruses from around the globe, and U2's "40," based on Psalm 40. The Old Testament reading from the lectionary is staged as a drama and liturgical dance, while the reading from the Gospel is backed up by a soulful anthem from the sax. The homily focuses on the Epistle, challenging the congregation to reorient their desires to what really matters (Phil. 1:9–10). This ultimately points us to two important communal experiences of our identity and opportunities for formation. First, this week a young family has brought their daughter to be baptized. Utilizing a beautiful baptismal formula from the sixteenth-century Huguenots, the parents express their desire and passion to see their daughter formed in the faith; but we too, as the congregation, pledge to be the village that will raise her together in Christ.[67] Second, baby Anthea, newly welcomed into the body of Christ, pulls up to the table with her family to participate in her first meal at Christ's table: the Eucharist. Anthea, with her siblings and parents, remain seated at the table. After the consecration of the meal (including a poem by Anne Sexton), the celebrant invites the congregation to share in Christ's body and blood by being seated at the table with Anthea, newest member of the church's family. Anthea's parents pour wine and break bread for each of us as we sit briefly at the table of fellowship and communion. As we proceed to and from the table, the ensemble has spread out around the sanctuary, and the sounds of the instruments bounce back and forth across the worship space. The digital glass has shifted to images of children from around our community—the local space that is our parish. We are reminded that our commitment to Anthea is both a communal commitment and a commitment to our community.

At the conclusion of worship, we are sent out into our neighborhood as ambassadors of the King-in-waiting, reminded of Monday's meeting about the neighborhood co-housing project, and reminded of our Sabbath commitment to abstain from the economic cycle for the day. The walk home with parishioners

67. See Tod Bolsinger, *It Takes a Church to Raise a Christian: How the Community of God Transforms Lives* (Grand Rapids: Brazos, 2004).

who are also neighbors solidifies the sense that we are a peculiar people.

The radically orthodox church, then, is not traditionalist, even if it is traditioned; it is not a rote system of repetition but a creative repetition of the core features of what constitutes us as the people of God; it is not a nostalgic retreat into "the way we used to do it" but a dynamic reappropriation of ancient practices as the very material means to be formed differently, as agents who will counter the practices of modernity's market and empire. The radically orthodox church is the space for the formation of postmodern catholics.

Annotated Bibliography

Further Reading on Postmodernism and Christian Faith

In this book we've only scratched the surface of thinking about the shape of Christian faith in postmodernity. For those interested in thinking about this further, here are some books that can help you along the way. Texts marked with an asterisk (*) are a little more technical.

Baker, Jonny, and Doug Gay, with Jenny Brown. *Alternative Worship: Resources from and for the Emerging Church.* Grand Rapids: Baker, 2004. A wonderful, unique book that provides concrete worship and liturgical resources for alternative worship that has "one hand in the past and one in the future." Includes a CD-ROM. An excellent resource.

*Benson, Bruce Ellis. *Graven Ideologies: Nietzsche, Derrida, and Marion on Modern Idolatry.* Downers Grove, IL: InterVarsity, 2002. A book that demonstrates the way postmodernism can be seen as a critique of idols and thus amenable to Christian faith.

Dawn, Marva. *Reaching Out without Dumbing Down: A Theology of Worship for This Urgent Time.* Grand Rapids: Eerdmans, 1995. Dawn tends to be critical of postmodernity but largely because she simply identifies it with modernity. She sees "seeker-sensitive" models of the church as postmodern, whereas I would say they are thoroughly modern. As a result, her suggestion of a rich liturgy as an antidote is, I suggest, postmodern.

Hauerwas, Stanley. *A Better Hope: Resources for a Church Confronting Capitalism, Democracy, and Postmodernity.* Grand Rapids: Brazos, 2000. I would recommend almost anything Hauerwas writes as relevant to the question of postmodernity, but here he addresses the question head-on. More accessible than you might think.

*Hughes, Graham. *Worship as Meaning: A Liturgical Theology for Late Modernity.* Cambridge: Cambridge University Press, 2003. This book considers the way in which worship weaves a symbolic web that both draws on and challenges the meanings available to us in late modernity.

Kitchens, Jim. *The Postmodern Parish: New Ministry for a New Era.* Herndon, VA: Alban Institute, 2003. An interesting book; sort of Brian McLaren meets Stanley Hauerwas.

McLaren, Brian D. *The Church on the Other Side: Doing Ministry in the Postmodern Matrix.* Grand Rapids: Zondervan, 2000. Though a bit glitzy in the way it hails postmodernity as a radically new era, this book takes up very specific strategies for the church to rethink itself in the contemporary world. In general, I wish McLaren's vision of the church were more sacramental (like Webber's), but this is still a helpful book.

———. *A Generous Orthodoxy: Why I Am a Missional, Evangelical, Post/Protestant, Liberal/Conservative, Mystical/Poetic, Biblical, Charismatic/Contemplative, Fundamentalist/Calvinist, Anabaptist/Anglican, Methodist, Catholic, Green, Incarnational, Depressed-Yet-Hopeful, Emergent, Unfinished Christian.* El Cajon, CA: Emergent Youth Specialties; Grand Rapids: Zondervan, 2004. This book offers theology in a confessional mode, honestly tackling the hard questions. Chapter 5, on the church as missional, is itself worth the price of the book.

———. *A New Kind of Christian: A Tale of Two Friends on a Spiritual Journey.* San Francisco: Jossey-Bass, 2001. This book, which generated some controversy, put the emerging church conversation on the map. It is written as a dialogue/novel and raises the grassroots questions of postmodernity, tackling doubt and anxiety head-on. Highly recommended, and a great book for small-group discussion. It has now been extended into a trilogy: *The Story We Find Ourselves In: Further Adventures of a New Kind of Christian* (San Francisco: Jossey-Bass, 2003) and *The Last Word and the Word after That: A Tale of Faith, Doubt, and a New Kind of Christianity* (San Francisco: Jossey-Bass, 2005).

Middleton, J. Richard, and Brian J. Walsh. *Truth Is Stranger Than It Used to Be: Biblical Faith in a Postmodern Age.* Downers Grove, IL: InterVarsity, 1995. From the authors of the classic *Transforming Vision: Shaping a Christian World View* (Downers Grove, IL: InterVarsity, 1984), this book is one of the first nuanced engagements with postmodernism. Very strong on biblical engagement.

Raschke, Carl. *The Next Reformation: Why Evangelicals Must Embrace Postmodernity.* Grand Rapids: Baker, 2004. An introduction to postmodern thought from a professional philosopher with extensive engagement in real-world ministry. One of the few books that specifically tackles both theory and practice.

*Smith, James K. A. *The Fall of Interpretation: Philosophical Foundations for a Creational Hermeneutic.* Downers Grove, IL: InterVarsity, 2000. In this book I explore Derrida (and others) in more detail and argue that interpretation is a constitutive (and therefore good) feature of being a creature.

*———. *Introducing Radical Orthodoxy: Mapping a Post-secular Theology.* Grand Rapids: Baker, 2004. This book will introduce you to an important sensibility in contemporary theology and at least point toward how it should make a difference for worship and discipleship.

Walsh, Brian J., and Sylvia C. Keesmaat. *Colossians Remixed: Subverting the Empire.* Downers Grove, IL: InterVarsity, 2004. An outstanding "anti-commentary" that shows the enduring relevance of the biblical narrative in the context of postmodernity. One of a kind.

Webber, Robert E. *Ancient-Future Faith: Rethinking Evangelicalism for a Postmodern World.* Grand Rapids: Baker, 1999. In this very readable book, Webber makes the case that I have suggested: that a truly postmodern church will be deeply historical (recovering its ancient heritage) and liturgical (activating the imagination through symbol and sacrament).

———. *The Younger Evangelicals: Facing the Challenges of the New World.* Grand Rapids: Baker, 2002. Here Webber provides a report on the state of the emerging church. He does so by showing the differences between traditional evangelicals, pragmatic evangelicals (seeker-sensitive), and younger evangelicals. Includes both diagnosis and prognosis with specific, concrete suggestions for worship, youth ministry, discipleship, the arts, and more. A great book.

Online Resources

As a complement to the annotated bibliography on postmodernism and Christian faith, here are some select Web-based resources for further exploring the shape of the church in postmodernity.[1]

The Ooze (http://www.theooze.com). This is "the" site for thinking about the emerging church. Includes articles that are regularly updated and organized under the categories of culture, faith, and ministry. Also provides information on new books, upcoming events, and opportunities to connect with others via online forums. Excellent design to boot.

Emergent (http://www.emergentvillage.com). Recently redesigned to be more clear and intuitive, it contains very helpful resources, including articles, online forums, and information about upcoming Emerging Gatherings, conferences, and other events, including online conferences and lectures. You can also sign up for an Emergent Village e-newsletter.

Ancient-Future Worship (http://www.ancientfutureworship .com). A site hosted by Robert Webber's Institute for Worship Studies that provides some resources for churches trying

1. Compiled by James K. A. Smith (http://www.jameskasmith.com).

to integrate the insights of *Ancient-Future Faith* into their worship.

Sacramentis.com (http://www.sacramentis.com). Hosted by Sally Morgenthaler, a leader in helping churches rethink worship in ways that are both ancient and postmodern. Lots of wisdom and some beautiful images on this site.

The Ekklesia Project (http://www.ekklesiaproject.org). The Ekklesia Project is an ecumenical, cross-denominational movement that seeks to think about a more radical understanding of being disciples of Jesus, emphasizing the church's countercultural calling. Lots of resources, including articles and an e-zine.

Journal for Cultural and Religious Theory (http://www.jcrt .org). This online journal provides access to some of the best work at the intersection of Continental philosophy, theology, and religious studies. Excellent design and rich archives.